WOMEN EMBRACING PEACE

Mindfulness and Meditation Practices to Release
Control, Reduce Stress, Regulate Emotions, and
Embrace Self-Compassion for Holistic Well-Being

EVE MEADOWS

Contents

Introduction

A few years ago, I sat in my car, gripping the steering wheel, tears streaming down my face. I had just left yet another stressful meeting where my perfectionism had been both my driving force and my undoing. I was exhausted, anxious, and overwhelmed. I realized that something had to change. This was my breaking point but also the beginning of a new journey. It was the moment I discovered mindfulness and meditation.

I started with small steps—pausing to take deep breaths, practicing gratitude, and eventually meditating for a few minutes each day. Slowly, I began to notice changes. My anxiety lessened, my need for control diminished, and I started to feel a sense of inner peace that I had never known before.

Many of us struggle with anxiety, perfectionism, and stress. We juggle multiple roles—mother, daughter, professional, friend—and often feel like we're failing. We set impossibly high standards for ourselves and feel crushed when we inevitably fall short. It's a cycle that can leave us feeling exhausted and inadequate.

That's where mindfulness and meditation come in. These practices offer a way to break the cycle. They help us find emotional balance, reduce stress, and overcome the crippling need for perfection. They teach us to be present in the moment and to accept ourselves just as we are.

The vision for "Women Embracing Peace" is to empower you to cultivate a life of emotional balance, inner calm, and self-acceptance through mindfulness practice. This book is not just another self-help guide. It's a supportive space to prioritize your emotional well-being, rediscover your inner strength, and find lasting peace.

This book is for you. Whether you are struggling with anxiety, feeling overwhelmed by the need for control, or constantly striving for perfection, this book is for you. It's for women who want to manage their mental health and embrace imperfection. It's for those who wish to release the need for control and find peace in the present moment.

The book is organized into several sections, each designed to guide you through different aspects of mindfulness and meditation. You'll find chapters on self-compassion, practical mindfulness techniques, emotional regulation, and living in the present moment. Each section includes personal stories, guided meditations, and real-life examples to help you apply these practices to your own life.

By working through this book, you will gain practical tools to manage your anxiety and stress. You will learn guided meditations to help you find calm and balance. You will read personal stories that show you are not alone in your struggles. You will find real-life examples demonstrating mindfulness's power in everyday life.

I encourage you to engage actively with this book. Try the exercises, reflect on the stories, and permit yourself to be imperfect. This journey is not about achieving perfection but finding peace and balance in imperfection.

So, dear reader, I invite you to join me on this journey towards inner peace and emotional resilience. Together, we will explore the power of mindfulness and meditation. We will uncover the strength within ourselves, embrace our imperfections, and find peace in the present moment.

Welcome to "Women Embracing Peace." Let's begin this journey together.

ONE

Embracing Self-Compassion

I remember a time when I was my harshest critic. I would look in the mirror and only see flaws. Every mistake felt like a monumental failure, and I carried the constant weight of not being good enough. During one particularly tough period, after a string of sleepless nights and countless bouts of self-doubt, I stumbled upon the concept of self-compassion. It was a lifeline I didn't know I needed. Self-compassion transformed my relationship with myself and, as a result, my entire life. Now, I want to share this powerful tool with you.

Understanding Self-Compassion

Self-compassion is about treating yourself with the same kindness and understanding you would offer a close friend. It involves three key components: self-kindness, common humanity, and mindfulness. Self-kindness means being gentle and understanding with yourself rather than harshly critical. Common humanity involves recognizing that everyone makes mistakes and has flaws.

Finally, mindfulness requires being present with your feelings and thoughts without over-identifying or pushing them away.

You might wonder how self-compassion differs from self-esteem. While self-esteem is about evaluating yourself positively, often compared to others, self-compassion isn't about judging yourself. It's about embracing yourself as you are, imperfections and all. This difference is crucial because self-esteem can sometimes lead to narcissism or an inflated sense of self-importance. In contrast, self-compassion fosters a balanced view of oneself, free from the extremes of self-criticism or self-importance.

The psychological benefits of self-compassion are profound. Research by Dr. Kristin Neff, a pioneer in the field, shows that self-compassion is linked to lower levels of anxiety and depression. It enhances emotional resilience, helping you bounce back from setbacks more easily. Neff's studies also reveal that self-compassionate people tend to have healthier relationships and a greater sense of well-being. They're more likely to engage in constructive behaviors and less likely to suffer from stress-related issues.

For example, one study found that self-compassionate individuals are better at handling failure. Instead of spiraling into self-loathing, they acknowledge their mistakes and move forward. This approach reduces the emotional toll of failure and encourages a growth mindset. Another study showed that self-compassion can improve mental health by reducing rumination, which is the tendency to dwell on negative thoughts. By practicing self-compassion, you can break the cycle of negative thinking and cultivate a more positive and balanced mental state.

Despite its benefits, self-compassion is often misunderstood. One common myth is that self-compassion is a form of self-pity. However, self-compassion is the opposite of self-pity. While self-pity involves wallowing in your problems and feeling isolated, self-compassion involves recognizing your struggles and acknowledging that everyone experiences difficulties. This recognition fosters a sense of connection rather than isolation.

Another misconception is that self-compassion will make you lazy or complacent. In reality, self-compassion motivates you to improve yourself healthily. Treating yourself with kindness makes you more likely to take care of your health, set realistic goals, and pursue your passions. Self-compassion encourages you to strive for excellence without the fear of failure that perfectionism brings.

Some people believe that self-compassion is selfish. They worry that focusing on their own needs will make them neglect others. However, self-compassion enhances your ability to care for others. When you meet your own emotional needs, you're less likely to experience burnout and more able to offer genuine support to those around you. Self-compassion builds a foundation of emotional stability from which you can better connect with and help others.

Take a moment to reflect on your current level of self-compassion. How do you typically respond to your own mistakes or shortcomings? Are you kind to yourself, or tend to be overly critical? Consider keeping a journal to explore these questions. Write about a recent situation where you were hard on yourself and think about how you could respond with more self-compassion in the future.

You might find it helpful to write about your feelings and reactions in detail. Journaling can help you identify patterns in your self-talk and offer insights into how you treat yourself. Reflect on whether your self-criticism is helping or hindering you. Often, we find that harsh self-criticism only adds to our stress and anxiety, while self-compassion opens the door to healing and growth.

By understanding and practicing self-compassion, you can transform your relationship with yourself and learn to navigate life's challenges with greater ease and resilience. This chapter will guide you through this transformative process, offering practical tools and insights to help you embrace self-compassion and unlock your inner peace.

Breaking Free from Perfectionism

Perfectionism is a sneaky companion. It often wears the mask of ambition and high standards, but underneath, it harbors a relentless inner critic. Recognizing perfectionist tendencies in your thoughts and behaviors is the first step toward breaking free. You might find yourself constantly setting unrealistically high expectations, feeling a persistent fear of failure, or being overly critical of your performance. Perfectionists often procrastinate, not wanting to start a task unless they can do it perfectly, and they frequently seek validation from others. These tendencies are not just quirks; they are deeply ingrained habits that can contribute to chronic anxiety.

The connection between perfectionism and anxiety is well-documented. When you set impossible standards for yourself, you create a fertile ground for anxiety to flourish. Perfectionism feeds a cycle of stress and self-doubt. You might constantly worry about making mistakes, which leads to a heightened state of alertness and stress. This anxiety, in turn, reinforces the need to be perfect, creating a vicious loop. Consider the example of a woman who spends hours perfecting a presentation. Despite her efforts, she feels it's never good enough and stays up late, tweaking it until she's exhausted. This constant striving for perfection leaves her feeling drained and anxious, never satisfied with her work.

The costs of perfectionism are steep. Emotionally, it can lead to burnout, inadequacy, and persistent dissatisfaction. Perfectionism can strain personal relationships as well. Holding yourself to impossible standards might inadvertently project those expectations onto others, leading to frustration and conflict. Professionally, perfectionism can be equally damaging. It can cause you to miss deadlines due to excessive work refining or avoid taking on new challenges for fear of failing to meet your high standards. Physically, the stress associated with perfectionism can manifest as headaches, insomnia, or other stress-related ailments.

Overcoming perfectionism requires practical strategies and a shift in mindset. One effective approach is setting realistic goals. Instead of aiming for perfection, set achievable and specific goals. Break tasks into smaller, manageable steps and celebrate progress rather than perfection. Embrace mistakes as learning opportunities. Understand that making mistakes is a natural part of growth and development. Each mistake teaches a valuable lesson that can guide you toward improvement. Practicing self-forgiveness is crucial. When you fall short of your expectations, offer words of kindness and understanding instead of berating yourself, recognizing that it's okay to be imperfect.

Let me share some inspiring stories of women who have successfully overcome perfectionism through self-compassion. One high-achieving executive used to lose sleep over every minor error in her reports. By learning to set realistic goals and practicing self-forgiveness, she found a balance that allowed her to excel without burning out. She began to see mistakes as opportunities for growth rather than as failures. Another woman, a dedicated teacher, struggled with perfectionism in her classroom. She felt she had to be the perfect teacher to earn her students' respect. By embracing self-compassion, she learned to accept her imperfections and focus on the joy of teaching rather than the pressure of perfection.

In the workplace, perfectionism can be particularly challenging. I remember working with a colleague who was a textbook perfectionist. She would spend countless hours on projects, often missing deadlines because she was never satisfied with her work. This led to immense stress and strained relationships with her team. She learned to manage her perfectionist tendencies through self-compassion and setting realistic goals. She started to delegate tasks, trust her team, and accept that "good enough" was often more effective than perfect. This shift improved her well-being and enhanced her productivity and team dynamics.

I have battled with perfectionism in various facets of life. I used to believe everything had to be flawless before I could consider it complete. Whether it was a work project, a home improvement task, or even writing this book, the pressure to be perfect was relentless. It wasn't until I started practicing self-compassion that I realized the toll perfectionism was taking on my mental and physical health. By setting realistic goals and embracing my imperfections, I found a sense of peace and fulfillment that perfectionism could never offer. The journey is ongoing, but each step toward self-compassion brings more balance and joy into my life.

Cultivating a Kind Inner Voice

We all have an inner critic. That nagging voice tells you you must be better, smart, or capable enough. This inner critic can be relentless, undermining your self-worth and your confidence. Understanding this inner critic is the first step in transforming it into a kinder, more supportive voice.

The inner critic often has distinct characteristics. It's judgmental, harsh, and unforgiving. It thrives on comparing you to others and magnifying your flaws. This critical voice usually originates from early experiences, perhaps from critical parents, teachers, or societal expectations. Over time, these external critiques become internalized, forming a persistent negative self-talk that affects your self-worth.

The impact of the inner critic on self-worth can be profound. Constant self-criticism can lead to feelings of inadequacy and low self-esteem. It can make you doubt your abilities and hesitate to take risks. This negative self-talk can become a barrier to personal growth and happiness, trapping you in a cycle of self-doubt and discouragement.

But you can transform this negative self-talk into compassionate and supportive self-talk. The first step is identifying negative thought patterns. Pay attention to the language your inner critic uses. Is it filled with words like "always" and "never"? Does it focus on your failures and ignore your successes? Recognizing these patterns is crucial to changing them.

Once you've identified negative thoughts, work on reframing them. Instead of saying, "I always mess things up," try, "I made a mistake, but I can learn from it." Reframing helps shift the focus from self-blame to self-improvement. It's about turning critical thoughts into constructive ones that encourage growth rather than hinder it.

Practicing positive affirmations can also help. Positive affirmations are statements that reinforce positive beliefs about yourself. They might initially feel awkward, but with practice, they can become a powerful tool for transforming self-talk. Try affirmations like, "I am worthy of love and respect," or "I am capable and strong." Repeat them daily, and notice how they begin to shift your mindset.

Mindfulness is crucial in noticing self-critical thoughts and replacing them with kind words. Mindfulness involves observing your thoughts without judgment. When you practice mindfulness, you create a space between your thoughts and reactions, allowing you to choose a more compassionate response. One effective mindfulness technique is to simply observe your thoughts as they arise without getting caught up in them.

Exercises for practicing self-kindness in the moment can be incredibly helpful. When you notice self-critical thoughts, pause and take a few deep breaths. Remind yourself that it's okay to be imperfect. Place your hand on your heart and offer yourself words of kindness, just as you would to a dear friend. This simple gesture can help shift your mindset from self-criticism to self-compassion.

Incorporating daily mindfulness practices can also support a kinder inner voice. Set aside a few minutes each day for a mindfulness meditation. Focus on your breath and gently bring your attention back whenever your mind wanders. Over time, this practice can help you develop greater awareness of your thoughts and create a habit of self-compassion.

Practical Exercise: Loving-Kindness Meditation

One powerful exercise to cultivate a kind inner voice is the loving-kindness meditation. Find a quiet place where you won't be disturbed. Sit comfortably and close your eyes. Take a few deep breaths to center yourself. Begin by silently repeating loving-kind phrases to yourself, such as "May I be happy. May I be healthy. May I be safe. May I live with ease." Feel the warmth and compassion these words bring. After a few minutes, extend these wishes to others, starting with loved ones and gradually including neutral people and even difficult individuals. This practice can help develop a sense of compassion for yourself and others, fostering a kinder inner dialogue.

Another effective practice is self-compassion letter writing. Write a letter to yourself as if you were writing to a close friend who is struggling. Use kind and encouraging words. Acknowledge your struggles, but also remind yourself of your strengths and the progress you've made. This exercise can provide a tangible reminder of your self-worth and the importance of self-compassion.

Affirmation journaling is another great way to cultivate a kind inner voice. Each day, write down a few positive affirmations about yourself. Reflect on them and notice how they make you feel. Over time, this practice can help reinforce positive beliefs and diminish the inner critic's power.

By understanding and transforming your inner critic, you can cultivate a kind inner voice that supports your growth and well-being. This shift can profoundly impact your mental and emotional health, helping you navigate life with greater self-compassion and resilience.

Self-Compassion Exercises for Daily Life

Incorporating self-compassion into your daily routine can be a game-changer. Simple rituals and practices can create a foundation of kindness and understanding towards yourself. Let's explore practical ways to make self-compassion a part of your everyday life.

Daily Self-Compassion Rituals

Starting your day with self-compassion affirmations can set a positive tone. As you wake up each morning, speak kindly to yourself for a few moments. Say things like, "I am worthy of love and respect," or "I am enough, just as I am." These affirmations may initially feel strange, but with time, they can shift your mindset and help you approach the day with a compassionate heart.

In the evening, reflect on your day with a gratitude practice. As you lie in bed, think about three things you are grateful for. They can be small, like a warm cup of tea, or significant, like a supportive friend. This practice helps you end the day positively and reinforces self-compassion by focusing on the good in your life rather than what went wrong.

Midday self-check-ins are also crucial. During a busy day, pause to ask yourself how you're feeling. Are you stressed, tired, or anxious? Acknowledge these feelings without judgment and offer yourself some kindness. You might say, "It's okay to feel this way. I'm doing my best." This simple act of checking in can prevent stress and remind you to treat yourself compassionately.

Mindful Self-Compassion Practices

Taking self-compassion breaks throughout the day can help you stay grounded. Find a quiet space, close your eyes, and take a few deep breaths. Remind yourself that taking a break is okay and that your well-being matters. These short breaks can recharge your energy and provide peace on a hectic day.

Mindful breathing exercises are another powerful tool. When you feel overwhelmed, focus on your breath for a few minutes. Inhale deeply through your nose, hold for a few seconds, and exhale slowly through your mouth. This practice can calm your mind and body, allowing you to approach challenges with a clearer perspective.

A body scan for self-compassion can also be incredibly soothing. Lie comfortably and slowly bring your attention to each body part, starting from your toes and moving up to your head. As you focus on each area, send it kindness and gratitude. This practice helps you connect with your body and cultivate a sense of self-compassion.

Integrating Self-Compassion at Work

Work can be a breeding ground for stress and self-criticism. Practicing self-compassion in a professional setting is vital. Start by setting boundaries and learning to say no when necessary. It's okay to decline additional tasks if you're already overwhelmed. Saying no can be an act of self-compassion, allowing you to protect your well-being and maintain a healthy work-life balance.

In stressful situations, remind yourself to practice self-compassion. If you make a mistake or face criticism, take a moment to breathe and offer yourself understanding. Remember that everyone makes mistakes, and it's part of being human. A self-compassionate mindset can help you navigate challenges with resilience and grace.

Be a role model to encourage a self-compassionate work culture. Share your practices with colleagues and create an environment where it's okay to be imperfect. By showing kindness to yourself and others, you contribute to a supportive and compassionate workplace.

Building a Support System

Surrounding yourself with supportive people is crucial for fostering self-compassion. Identify individuals in your life who encourage and uplift you. These could be friends, family members, or colleagues who understand the importance of self-compassion and support your journey.

Setting healthy boundaries with unsupportive people is also essential. It's okay to distance yourself from those who bring negativity into your life. Protecting your emotional well-being is a form of self-compassion, and it's important to prioritize relationships that nourish you.

Creating a self-compassion support group can be incredibly beneficial. Find a few like-minded individuals who are also interested in practicing self-compassion. Meet regularly to share experiences, discuss challenges, and support each other. This group can provide a sense of community and accountability, making it easier to maintain your self-compassion practices.

Incorporating these self-compassion exercises into your daily life can transform how you treat yourself. By cultivating kindness and understanding, you can easily navigate challenges and foster inner peace. Remember, self-compassion is not a one-time act but a continuous practice that grows stronger. Embrace these practices and allow yourself to thrive.

TWO

Mindfulness Fundamentals

I remember a moment vividly from a few years ago. I was sitting in my living room, surrounded by a sea of papers and to-do lists. My mind was racing, my heart was pounding, and I felt like I was drowning in my own life. A friend mentioned mindfulness to me before, but I had brushed it off as another trend. But in that moment of overwhelming chaos, I decided to try it. I closed my eyes, took a deep breath, and focused on the feeling of the air filling my lungs. I felt a tiny spark of calm for the first time in what felt like forever. This was my first step into the world of mindfulness, and it changed everything.

What is Mindfulness?

Mindfulness is simply paying attention to the present moment without judgment. It sounds straightforward, but it's incredibly powerful. Rooted in Buddhist meditation practices, mindfulness has been around for thousands of years. These practices were designed to cultivate a deep awareness of the mind and body, helping practitioners live in harmony with themselves and the world around them.

In recent decades, mindfulness has been adapted into Western psychology. Researchers and therapists have recognized its benefits for mental health, integrating mindfulness into various therapeutic approaches. Programs like Mindfulness-Based Stress Reduction (MBSR) and Mindfulness-Based Cognitive Therapy (MBCT) have become popular tools for managing stress, anxiety, and depression. The beauty of mindfulness lies in its simplicity and accessibility—anyone can practice it anywhere, anytime.

At its core, mindfulness involves three principles: present-moment awareness, nonjudgmental observation, and acceptance. Present-moment awareness means focusing on what's happening now rather than dwelling on the past or worrying about the future. For example, when you're washing dishes, you might focus on the sensation of the warm water on your hands and the sound of the water splashing.

Non-judgmental observation involves noticing your thoughts, feelings, and sensations without labeling them good or bad. This can be challenging, especially if you're used to being self-critical. But with practice, you can learn to observe your inner experiences with curiosity and kindness. Imagine you're feeling anxious about an upcoming presentation. Instead of criticizing yourself for being nervous, you can simply acknowledge and observe the anxiety without judgment.

Acceptance is about letting go of the need to control everything and allowing things to be as they are. This doesn't mean giving up or being passive. Instead, it's about recognizing what you can't change and focusing your energy on what you can. For instance, if you're stuck in traffic and running late, you can accept the situation and use the time to practice mindful breathing rather than getting frustrated.

Many people confuse mindfulness with meditation, but they're not quite the same. Meditation is a broader practice that includes various techniques for calming the mind and achieving a state of deep relaxation or heightened awareness. Mindfulness is a specific type of meditation that focuses on present-moment awareness. While all mindfulness practices are a form of meditation, not all meditation practices are mindfulness-based.

There are countless ways to practice mindfulness beyond traditional meditation. Mindful walking is one example. Instead of rushing from place to place, try walking slowly and paying attention to each step. Notice the sensation of your feet touching the ground, the rhythm of your breath, and the sights and sounds around you. This simple practice can transform an ordinary walk into a calming, grounding experience.

Mindful listening is another powerful practice. Focus fully on the other person without planning your response or getting distracted when conversing. Listen with an open heart and mind, and notice how this deepens your connection with the other person. This practice enhances your relationships and brings a sense of presence and calm to your interactions.

Mindful eating is a practice that can transform your relationship with food. Instead of eating on autopilot, take the time to savor each bite. Notice the flavors, textures, and aromas of your food. Pay attention to how your body feels as you eat, and stop when satisfied. This practice can help you develop a healthier, more mindful approach to eating and reduce stress around food.

Incorporating mindfulness into your daily activities can profoundly impact your well-being. You don't need to set aside a specific time for mindfulness; you can weave it into your everyday life. Whether brushing your teeth, drinking tea, or folding laundry, you can practice mindfulness by focusing fully on the task.

By understanding and practicing mindfulness, you can find peace and balance amid life's challenges. It's a powerful tool for managing anxiety, controlling perfectionist tendencies, and cultivating inner peace. So, take a deep breath, and let's explore the transformative power of mindfulness together.

The Science Behind Mindfulness

The benefits of mindfulness are anecdotal and backed by solid scientific evidence. Harvard researchers, for instance, have been delving into the effects of mindfulness on brain function. Their studies show that mindfulness can bring about significant changes in the brain, particularly in areas associated with emotional regulation and stress. Functional magnetic resonance imaging (fMRI) scans reveal that regular mindfulness practice can reduce activity in the amygdala, the part of the brain responsible for our fight-or-flight response. This reduction in activity translates to lower stress levels and a calmer state of mind.

Moreover, the research continues beyond there. Studies have shown that mindfulness can enhance activity in the prefrontal cortex, the area of the brain responsible for executive functions like decision-making, focus, and self-control. This enhancement helps you stay more present and make better decisions, reducing the chaos that often fuels anxiety and perfectionism. Neuroscientific evidence also points to neuroplasticity, the brain's ability to reorganize itself by forming new neural connections. Mindfulness practices can promote neuroplasticity, making adopting healthier habits and thought patterns easier.

When it comes to health benefits, mindfulness offers a range of advantages. Scientific research has demonstrated that mindfulness can help reduce chronic pain. By teaching you to observe pain without judgment, mindfulness allows you to change your relationship with it, reducing its intensity. Studies also indicate that mindfulness can boost your immune function. A stronger immune system means you're less likely to fall ill, which can be a game-changer if you constantly battle stress-related ailments. Additionally, mindfulness is known to improve sleep quality. Better sleep leads to better overall health, making it easier to manage anxiety and stress.

The psychological benefits of mindfulness are equally compelling. Numerous studies have shown that mindfulness can significantly decrease symptoms of depression and anxiety. By fostering a non-judgmental awareness of your thoughts and feelings, mindfulness helps you break the cycle of negative thinking that often accompanies these conditions. Emotional resilience is another key benefit. Mindfulness practices teach you to observe your emotions without getting swept away, allowing you to respond to challenges more effectively. This increased emotional resilience can make a world of difference when dealing with the pressures of daily life.

Moreover, mindfulness can contribute to an overall sense of well-being. When you're more present and less worried about the past or future, you can better enjoy the moments that make life meaningful. This heightened well-being can enhance relationships, improve work performance, and make everyday activities more enjoyable. It's not just about reducing stress; it's about holistically enriching your life.

The Harvard Gazette reports that public interest in mindfulness has skyrocketed, and for good reason. Mindfulness-based interventions (MBIs) are increasingly used to treat a variety of psychological conditions, from stress and anxiety to chronic pain and depression. A growing body of research supports these interventions and highlights their effectiveness. For instance, MBIs have been shown to improve emotion regulation by enhancing both top-down and bottom-up mechanisms. This dual approach helps you manage your emotions more effectively, reducing the likelihood of emotional outbursts or prolonged periods of distress.

Neuroscientific studies also reveal that mindfulness impacts several brain regions involved in attention, emotional regulation, and self-referential processing. These include the insula, responsible for body awareness, and the anterior cingulate cortex, which plays a role in emotion regulation. By practicing mindfulness, you can change the structure and function of your brain, making it easier to manage stress and maintain emotional balance.

Regarding practical applications, mindfulness training modifies neural processes in the three attention networks: alerting, orienting, and executive control. This modification helps you stay focused and attentive, making managing tasks easier and reducing the overwhelm that often accompanies perfectionism. The changes in brain function are not just temporary; they persist even when you're not actively meditating. This means that the benefits of mindfulness extend beyond your practice sessions, enriching your daily life in meaningful ways.

So, let's talk about how all this scientific evidence translates into real-world benefits. Imagine you're at work, juggling multiple deadlines, and feeling the pressure to perform perfectly. Mindfulness can activate your prefrontal cortex, helping you stay focused and make better decisions. This can reduce your stress levels and improve your performance, making it easier to meet your deadlines without feeling overwhelmed. Or consider a situation where you're dealing with chronic pain. Mindfulness can help you observe the pain without judgment, reducing its intensity and making it easier to cope.

The Benefits of Mindful Living

When you start embracing mindfulness, one of the first things you may notice is an improvement in your emotional well-being. Mindfulness helps you regulate your emotions more effectively, making navigating life's ups and downs easier. Techniques like mindful breathing and body scans can help you observe your emotions without getting swept away. For instance, when you feel a wave of anxiety coming on, instead of letting it take over, you can take a moment to focus on your breath, acknowledging the anxiety without judgment. This simple practice can create a space between you and your emotions, allowing you to respond more calmly and thoughtfully.

Let's look at some real-life examples. Take Jamie, a high-powered executive who struggled with stress and anxiety. After incorporating mindfulness into her daily routine, she was less reactive and more composed during high-stress meetings. She began to use mindful breathing techniques whenever she felt overwhelmed, which helped her maintain her composure and make better decisions. Similarly, a teacher, Mikayla, used mindfulness to manage her stress levels during the school day. She could stay grounded and present by taking short mindfulness breaks between classes, improving her interactions with students and colleagues.

Mindfulness also significantly enhances focus and concentration, benefiting your personal and professional life. Training your mind to stay in the present moment can reduce distractions and improve your ability to concentrate on tasks. One simple exercise to improve concentration is the practice of mindful observation. Pick an object, like a flower or a piece of fruit, and spend a few minutes observing it in detail. Notice its colors, textures, and shapes. This exercise can help train your mind to focus and is particularly helpful if you struggle with maintaining attention at work.

Consider the case of Katelyn, a writer who found it challenging to focus on her projects due to constant distractions. She improved her concentration and productivity by integrating mindfulness practices into her routine. She started her day with a short meditation session and used mindful breaks to reset her focus. This practice not only boosted her productivity but also enhanced the quality of her work. Similarly, Meghan, a software engineer, used mindfulness to improve her focus during coding sessions. She could work more efficiently and clearly by practicing mindful breathing before starting her tasks.

Enhanced relationships are another significant benefit of mindful living. Mindfulness fosters empathy, active listening, and emotional understanding, which are crucial for healthy relationships. Mindful communication techniques, such as active listening and non-judgmental observation, can improve your interactions with others. When you practice mindful communication, you focus entirely on the other person, listening to their words without planning your response or getting distracted. This deep level of attentiveness can strengthen your connections and improve your relationships.

Take the example of Brooke and her husband struggling with communication issues. By incorporating mindfulness practices into their interactions, they improved their understanding of each other's perspectives. They practiced active listening during their conversations, which helped them feel more connected and supported. Similarly, Danielle used mindfulness to improve her relationship with her teenage daughter. She created a more open and supportive environment for their conversations by practicing non-judgmental observation and empathy.

The overall quality of life also improves when you embrace mindful living. Mindfulness helps you find balance and fulfillment in your daily activities, making life more enjoyable and meaningful. Testimonials from individuals who practice mindfulness often highlight its profound impact on their overall well-being. For example, a busy professional, Sidney found that mindfulness helped her achieve a better work-life balance. By incorporating mindfulness into her daily routine, she was able to reduce stress and find more joy in his personal life.

Practical tips for integrating mindfulness into daily life can make a significant difference. Start by setting aside a few minutes each day for mindfulness practice. You can begin with short sessions and gradually increase the duration as you become more comfortable. Incorporate mindfulness into everyday activities, such as eating, walking, or household chores. The key is to be fully present in whatever you are doing, focusing on the sensations and experiences of the moment.

By embracing mindful living, you can enhance your emotional well-being, improve your focus and concentration, foster healthier relationships, and achieve a higher overall quality of life. Mindfulness is not just a practice; it's a way of living that can transform every aspect of your life. So take a deep breath, be present, and start experiencing the countless benefits of mindful living today.

Dispelling Myths About Mindfulness

One common misconception is that mindfulness is inherently religious. While it's true that mindfulness has historical roots in Buddhist meditation practices, it has been adapted into a secular context that makes it accessible to everyone. In its modern form, mindfulness is about paying attention to the present moment without judgment and doesn't require any particular spiritual belief. Secular mindfulness programs like Mindfulness-Based Stress Reduction (MBSR) and Mindfulness-Based Cognitive Therapy (MBCT) have been developed to help people manage stress, anxiety, and other mental health issues. These programs are used in hospitals, schools, and workplaces worldwide, making mindfulness a universal tool for well-being. Testimonials from people of diverse spiritual backgrounds show that mindfulness can complement various belief systems rather than conflict with them. Whether you're religious, spiritual, or neither, mindfulness offers practical benefits that anyone can enjoy.

Another myth is that mindfulness requires a lot of time. Many people think they must dedicate hours daily to practice mindfulness effectively, but this isn't true. Even brief practices can be incredibly effective. You can start with just five minutes a day. Simple exercises like mindful breathing or a quick body scan can fit easily into your busy schedule. Take, for instance, a working mom named Tenisha who juggles a demanding job and two kids. She found that practicing mindfulness for just a few minutes in the morning and evening significantly impacted her stress levels. Tips for integrating mindfulness into a busy schedule include setting reminders on your phone, practicing mindfulness during daily activities like brushing your teeth or waiting in line, and taking short, mindful breaks throughout the day. The key is consistency, not duration. Small, regular practices can lead to meaningful changes over time.

Many people also believe mindfulness is about clearing your mind of all thoughts. This is a misconception. Mindfulness is not about emptying your mind but observing your thoughts without judgment. It's natural for your mind to wander; the goal is to notice where it goes and gently bring it back to the present moment. Understanding the nature of thoughts can help you practice non-judgmental observation. Your thoughts are just mental events—they come and go like clouds in the sky. Techniques for non-judgmental observation include focusing on your breath, labeling your thoughts (e.g., "thinking" or "worrying"), and using a gentle, curious attitude toward your mental experiences. Personal stories of practicing mindful observation show that this approach can reduce the power of negative thoughts and increase emotional resilience. For example, Teresa, who struggled with chronic anxiety, found that observing her anxious thoughts without judgment helped her feel less overwhelmed and more in control.

Another myth is that mindfulness is only for naturally calm or serene individuals. This couldn't be further from the truth. Mindfulness is especially beneficial for people who experience high levels of stress or anxiety. It provides tools to navigate life's challenges with greater ease. Examples of high-stress individuals benefiting from mindfulness include first responders, military personnel, and busy professionals.

These people often face intense pressure and stress, yet mindfulness helps them stay grounded and focused. Techniques for practicing mindfulness amidst chaos include grounding exercises, mindful breathing, and using mindfulness apps to guide you through quick practices. Encouraging stories of transformation through mindfulness shows that it can bring significant benefits even in the most chaotic environments. Take Jenna, a nurse working in a busy hospital. Practicing mindfulness taught her to stay calm and centered during emergencies, improving her performance and reducing her stress levels.

By dispelling these myths, we open the door for everyone to experience the transformative power of mindfulness. It's not about adhering to a particular belief system, dedicating hours of your day, or achieving a state of thoughtless bliss. Mindfulness is for everyone, especially those navigating the complexities of modern life. With its practical applications and proven benefits, mindfulness can help you manage anxiety, control perfectionist tendencies, and find inner peace. In the next chapter, we'll delve into practical mindfulness techniques you can use immediately. These tools will help you integrate mindfulness into your daily routine, making it a natural part of your life.

THREE

Practical Mindfulness Techniques

Let's dive into some practical mindfulness techniques to help you manage anxiety, control, and perfectionism while deepening your inner peace.

Mindful Breathing Exercises

It all started with a breath. I remember one particularly chaotic day when everything seemed to spiral out of control. I felt like I was sinking into a sea of stress and anxiety. That's when a friend suggested I try mindful breathing. Skeptical but desperate, I decided to give it a shot. I closed my eyes, took a deep breath, and focused on the sensation of air filling my lungs. Something shifted within me. That single breath became an anchor, grounding me in the present moment and offering a brief respite from my racing thoughts.

Mindful breathing is the cornerstone of mindfulness practice. It involves paying attention to your breath, observing each inhale and exhale without trying to change it. The beauty of mindful breathing lies in its simplicity and accessibility. You don't need any special equipment or a quiet room. All you need is your breath, which is always with you. The basics of mindful breathing are straightforward: find a comfortable position, close your eyes if you feel comfortable, and focus on the sensation of breathing. Notice the cool air entering your nostrils and the warm air leaving. Feel your chest and belly rise and fall with each breath. If your mind wanders, gently bring it back to your breath without judgment.

Mindful breathing can significantly reduce stress and anxiety. When you focus on your breath, you bring your attention to the present moment, which can help break the cycle of anxious thoughts. Physiologically, mindful breathing activates the parasympathetic nervous system, which promotes relaxation. Deep, slow breaths signal to your body that it's safe to relax, reducing the production of stress hormones like cortisol. This physiological response can help lower your heart rate and blood pressure, creating a sense of calm and grounding.

Let's explore a few simple breathing techniques you can practice anytime, anywhere. The 4-7-8 breathing technique is a favorite of mine. It's simple yet powerful. Here's how it works: inhale through your nose for a count of four, hold your breath for seven, and exhale through your mouth for a count of eight. Repeat this cycle three to four times. This technique can help calm your mind and body, making it easier to manage anxiety and stress.

Another effective technique is box breathing, also known as square breathing. This method involves inhaling, holding, exhaling, and holding your breath again, each for a count of four. Imagine tracing the sides of a square as you breathe: inhale for four counts, hold for four, exhale for four, and hold again for four. This rhythmic breathing pattern can help regulate your breath and create a sense of balance and calm.

Alternate nostril breathing is a technique often used in yoga. It involves breathing in and out of one nostril at a time, alternating between them. Start by sitting comfortably. Close your right nostril with your right thumb and inhale deeply through your left nostril. Close your left nostril with your right ring finger and exhale through your right nostril. Inhale through your right nostril, then close it and exhale through your left nostril. Continue this pattern for a few minutes. Alternate nostril breathing can help balance your brain's left and right hemispheres, promoting mental clarity and emotional stability.

Deep breathing exercises can also help with relaxation and grounding. The diaphragm plays a crucial role in deep breathing. When you breathe deeply from your diaphragm rather than shallowly from your chest, you can access a deeper state of relaxation. To practice deep belly breathing, sit or lie down comfortably. Place one hand on your chest and the other on your belly. Take a slow, deep breath through your nose, allowing your belly to rise and push your hand out. Your chest should remain relatively still. Exhale slowly through your mouth, feeling your belly fall. Repeat this process for a few minutes, focusing on the rise and fall of your belly.

Integrating mindful breathing into your daily life can be incredibly beneficial. You can practice mindful breathing during work breaks to reset and recharge. Take a few minutes to step away from your desk, find a quiet spot, and focus on your breath. This can help you return to your tasks with renewed focus and calm. Using mindful breathing to start and end your day can also set a positive tone. Begin your morning with a few minutes of mindful breathing to center yourself before the day begins. Use mindful breathing to unwind and prepare for a restful sleep at night.

Mindful breathing can be a powerful tool to regain composure during stressful situations. If you find yourself feeling overwhelmed, take a moment to focus on your breath. Even a few deep, mindful breaths can create a sense of calm and help you navigate the situation with clarity and poise.

Practice Exercise: Quick Mindful Breathing Break

Take a moment right now to practice a quick, mindful breathing break. Find a comfortable position and close your eyes if you feel comfortable. Take a deep breath through your nose, allowing your belly to rise. Hold the breath for a count of three, then exhale slowly through your mouth, letting your belly fall. Repeat this process three times. Notice how you feel before and after the exercise. This quick break can be used anytime during your day to center yourself and find peace.

Mindful breathing is a simple yet powerful practice that can help you manage anxiety, control, and perfectionism. Incorporating these techniques into your daily life can create calm and grounding moments, deepening your inner peace.

Body Scan Meditation

It was one of those nights where sleep seemed impossible. My mind was racing, and my body was tense from the day's stress. I remembered hearing about body scan meditation from a mindfulness workshop I had attended, so I decided to try it. I lay down, closed my eyes, and focused on different body parts, starting from my toes and moving up to my head. As I paid attention to each area, I noticed the tension melting away and a sense of calm washing over me. That night, I slept better than I had in weeks.

Body scan meditation is a powerful technique that involves paying close attention to various parts of your body, one at a time. The purpose is to develop a greater mind-body connection, enhancing your awareness of physical sensations and how they relate to your mental and emotional state. This practice can help you identify areas of tension or discomfort, allowing you to address them before they escalate. The benefits of body scan meditation are numerous. It can significantly reduce stress and promote relaxation, making it easier to manage anxiety and perfectionist tendencies. You can cultivate a deeper inner peace and well-being by focusing on the present moment and observing your body's sensations without judgment.

To enhance the effectiveness of your body scan meditation, create a quiet and comfortable environment. Find a space where you won't be disturbed, and consider using soft lighting or calming scents like lavender to set the mood. Setting a regular practice schedule can also be beneficial. Consistency is key to reaping the full benefits of mindfulness practices. Aim to practice body scan meditation at the same time each day, whether in the morning to start your day calmly or in the evening to unwind before bed. Guided body scan recordings can be helpful, especially if you're new to the practice. Many apps and online resources offer guided meditations, providing gentle prompts to help you stay focused and present.

Body scan meditation can address common challenges in various real-life scenarios. For instance, it's an excellent tool for reducing tension and pain. If you experience chronic pain or muscle tension, regular body scan practice can help you become more aware of these sensations and manage them more effectively. It can also improve sleep quality. By practicing body scan meditation before bed, you can release the day's stress and prepare your mind and body for restful sleep. Additionally, body scan meditation can enhance focus and concentration. When you develop a habit of tuning into your body's sensations, you can carry this heightened awareness into other areas of your life, improving your ability to stay present and focused on tasks.

Practice Exercise: Body Scan Meditation

Find a quiet place where you won't be disturbed. Lie down or sit comfortably, and close your eyes. Take a few deep breaths to center yourself. Start by focusing on your toes. Notice any sensations, whether it's warmth, coolness, or tingling. Allow yourself to observe these sensations without judgment. Slowly move your attention up to your feet, then to your ankles, calves, knees, and so on, until you've scanned your entire body from head to toe. As you move through each part of your body, practice observing sensations without judgment. If you notice tension or discomfort, breathe into that area and visualize the tension melting away with each exhale. This practice can help you develop a more compassionate relationship with your body, recognizing that it's okay to experience discomfort and that you can address it mindfully.

Body scan meditation is a versatile and effective mindfulness practice that can help you manage anxiety, control, and perfectionism. Incorporating this technique into your daily routine can deepen your connection with your body, reduce stress, and cultivate inner peace.

Walking Meditation for Busy Lives

I remember when my days were so packed that finding a moment to sit quietly felt impossible. One day, a mentor suggested walking meditation—a revolutionary practice. Instead of trying to carve out time to sit still, I could integrate mindfulness into something I was already doing: walking. Walking meditation is a practice that combines the physical act of walking with the mental focus of meditation. It allows you to bring your body and mind into sync, creating a harmonious rhythm that can be incredibly grounding.

Walking meditation offers numerous benefits for both mental and physical health. It can reduce stress, improve mood, and enhance focus, much like traditional seated meditation. However, walking meditation also provides the added advantage of physical exercise. This makes it an excellent choice for busy individuals struggling to find time for physical activity and mindfulness. Walking meditation can be practiced almost anywhere, unlike seated meditation, which requires a quiet space and a certain amount of stillness. Walking through a bustling city or a tranquil park, you can transform your steps into a meditative practice.

To perform walking meditation, start by finding a suitable location. It could be a quiet path, a section of your office building, or even a hallway at home. The key is choosing a place to walk back and forth without too many distractions. Begin by standing still momentarily, taking a few deep breaths to center yourself. As you start walking, focus on the sensations of each step. Feel your feet touching the ground, notice the movement of your legs, and pay attention to the rhythm of your gait. Try to synchronize your breath with your steps. For example, inhale for four steps, then exhale for the next four. This rhythmic breathing can help you stay focused and present.

Incorporating walking meditation into your daily routine can be surprisingly easy. One effective way is to practice it during your daily commute. If you walk to work or use public transportation, focus on your steps and breath for a few minutes. This can transform a mundane commute into a calming, mindful experience. Using walking meditation during work breaks is another excellent option. Instead of scrolling through your phone or grabbing a coffee, take a short walk around your office building or nearby park. This practice can help clear your mind and improve your focus for the rest of the day. Combining walking meditation with nature walks can also be profoundly grounding. The natural environment can enhance your sense of presence and connection, making the practice even more powerful.

The broader concept of mindful movement extends beyond walking meditation, including activities like yoga and tai chi. These practices incorporate mindfulness into physical exercise, offering a holistic approach to well-being. Yoga, for example, combines physical postures with mindful breathing and meditation, promoting flexibility, strength, and mental clarity. Tai chi, a form of martial arts, emphasizes slow, deliberate movements and focused attention, making it a moving meditation. Incorporating mindful movement into your exercise routines can enhance physical and mental health.

Personal stories of transformation through mindful movement are inspiring. Take, for example, a friend of mine who struggled with chronic stress and anxiety. She began incorporating yoga into her daily routine, focusing on breathing and movement. Over time, she noticed a significant reduction in her anxiety levels and an improvement in her overall mood. Another example is a colleague practicing tai chi to manage work-related stress. The slow, rhythmic movements helped her stay present and calm, even during high-pressure situations. These stories highlight the transformative power of mindful movement in everyday life.

Practice Exercise: Walking Meditation

Find a quiet place where you can walk back and forth without distractions. Stand still momentarily, taking a few deep breaths to center yourself. As you start walking, focus on the sensations of each step. Feel your feet touching the ground, notice the movement of your legs, and pay attention to the rhythm of your gait. Try to synchronize your breath with your steps, inhaling for four steps and exhaling for four. Continue walking mindfully for five to ten minutes, observing any changes in your mind and body. This practice can be easily integrated into your daily routine, offering peace and grounding amidst your busy schedule.

Mindful Eating Practices

Mindful eating is a practice that goes beyond simply nourishing your body. It's about engaging all your senses and being fully present during your meals. Mindful eating means paying close attention to the experience of eating without judgment. It involves savoring each bite, noticing your food's colors, textures, and flavors, and truly appreciating the act of eating. By doing so, you not only enhance your dining experience but also improve your digestion and satisfaction levels. Eating mindfully allows your body to signal hunger and fullness cues more effectively, helping you avoid overeating and promoting better digestion.

The principles of mindful eating are rooted in mindfulness, which means focusing on the present moment. This can significantly impact your relationship with food. For instance, when you eat mindlessly, you might eat quickly, barely taste your food, or eat while distracted by TV or work. In contrast, mindful eating encourages you to slow down and appreciate each bite. This can lead to greater satisfaction and enjoyment, making your meals more fulfilling both physically and emotionally.

Mindful eating also offers psychological benefits. It can help reduce stress and anxiety around food, making mealtime a more relaxing and enjoyable experience. By being present and fully engaged with your food, you can cultivate a healthier relationship with eating, free from guilt or anxiety. This practice can also help you become more attuned to your body's needs, allowing you to make more conscious and nourishing food choices.

Practicing mindful eating involves a few simple techniques. Start by eating slowly and savoring each bite. Take the time to chew your food thoroughly, noticing its texture and flavor. This not only enhances your eating experience but also aids digestion. Pay attention to the colors, textures, and tastes of your food. Notice the vibrant colors of vegetables, the smooth texture of yogurt, or the crunch of a fresh apple. Engaging your senses in this way can make each meal a more immersive and enjoyable experience.

Listening to your body's hunger and fullness cues is another crucial aspect of mindful eating. Before you start eating, take a moment to check in with your body. Are you truly hungry or eating out of habit or emotion? Throughout the meal, pause occasionally to assess your level of fullness. This can help you avoid overeating and make more conscious food choices. By tuning into your body's signals, you can eat in a way that truly nourishes you rather than simply filling a void.

Emotional eating is a common challenge that many of us face. We often use food for comfort during stress, sadness, or boredom. Mindful eating can help address these emotional eating habits by encouraging you to identify your emotional triggers for eating. When you feel the urge to eat, pause and ask yourself if you're truly hungry or trying to soothe an emotion. Practicing self-compassion during emotional eating episodes is essential. Acknowledge your feelings and offer yourself kindness instead of judging yourself for turning to food for comfort. This can help break the cycle of emotional eating and promote a healthier relationship with food.

Techniques for redirecting emotional eating behaviors include finding alternative ways to cope with your emotions. Instead of reaching for a snack when stressed, try taking a walk, practicing deep breathing, or calling a friend. These activities can provide the comfort and distraction you seek without the negative consequences of emotional eating. Over time, you can develop healthier coping mechanisms that support your overall well-being.

Integrating mindful eating into your daily life doesn't have to be complicated. Start by creating a calm and distraction-free eating environment. Turn off the TV, put away your phone, and focus solely on your meal. This can help you fully engage with your food and enjoy the experience. Setting intentions before meals can also be beneficial. Take a moment to express gratitude for your food and set an intention for mindful eating. This simple practice can help you approach your meals with mindfulness and appreciation.

Practicing gratitude for food and its sources is another powerful way to enhance your mindful eating practice. Before you begin eating, take a moment to reflect on the journey your food has taken to reach your plate. Consider the farmers who grew the produce, the workers who transported it, and the chefs who prepared it. This practice can deepen your appreciation for your food and make each meal a more meaningful experience.

Mindful eating is a powerful practice that can transform your relationship with food. Being fully present and engaged during meals can improve your digestion, reduce stress, and cultivate a healthier relationship with eating. As you incorporate these techniques into your daily life, mindful eating becomes a natural and enjoyable part of your routine.

Next, we'll explore how mindfulness techniques can help you manage anxiety and emotional regulation. These practices will provide you with tools to navigate life's challenges with greater ease and resilience.

FOUR

Managing Anxiety Through Mindfulness

I remember sitting in a crowded café, trying to enjoy a cup of coffee, when a sudden wave of anxiety hit me out of nowhere. My heart started racing, and my palms got sweaty. All I wanted was to bolt out of there. It was baffling because there was no apparent reason for my anxiety. This experience made me realize how crucial it is to understand what triggers these anxious episodes. Identifying these triggers is often the first step in managing anxiety effectively.

Identifying Anxiety Triggers

Anxiety triggers are specific events, situations, or even thoughts that cause your anxiety to spike. Understanding these triggers is like finding the key to a locked door. Once you identify them, you can manage and reduce their impact on your life. Common types of anxiety triggers include social situations, work stress, and even memories from past experiences. For instance, you might feel a rush of anxiety before giving a presentation at work or when you're in a crowded room. Sometimes, the trigger isn't as obvious—it could be a specific sound, smell, or even a fleeting thought that brings back a stressful memory. Past experiences, especially traumatic ones, can play a significant role in current anxiety. These experiences get stored in your brain and can resurface as anxiety triggers, even if you don't consciously remember them.

Becoming self-aware is crucial in identifying these triggers. One effective technique is journaling. Try keeping a journal to track your anxiety episodes. Whenever you feel anxious, jot down the details of the situation: where you were, what you were doing, and what thoughts were running through your mind. Over time, you may notice patterns. For example, you might realize that your anxiety spikes every Monday morning before work or whenever you have to attend a social gathering. This awareness can be incredibly empowering, as it gives you insight into what specifically triggers your anxiety.

Mindfulness meditation is another powerful tool for self-awareness. Set aside a few minutes daily to sit quietly and observe your thoughts and feelings without judgment. This practice can help you become more attuned to the subtle cues that indicate an anxiety trigger is present. For instance, you might notice a tightening in your chest or a racing heart whenever you think about an upcoming event. This heightened awareness can help you identify triggers you might not have been conscious of before. Daily reflection practices, like taking a few moments before bed to review your day, can also help you pinpoint what triggered your anxiety and how you responded to it.

Once you've started to identify your anxiety triggers, the next step is to analyze patterns. Keeping an anxiety log can be incredibly helpful for this. In your log, note down each anxiety episode along with the details of the situation. After a few weeks, review your log to identify any recurring themes or situations. You might notice that certain people, places, or activities consistently trigger your anxiety. For example, work-related stress is a significant trigger. Identifying these patterns can help you take proactive steps to manage your anxiety more effectively.

It is also essential to use mindfulness to notice subtle triggers. Sometimes, the triggers are not obvious and can be as subtle as a particular scent or a specific type of lighting. Mindfulness can help you become more aware of these subtle cues. For instance, you might realize that a particular perfume reminds you of a stressful event from your past, triggering anxiety. This awareness allows you to address the root cause of your anxiety rather than just its symptoms.

Practical Exercise: Guided Self-Reflection Questions

Take a moment to sit quietly with a journal and reflect on the following questions:

1. When was the last time you felt a sudden rush of anxiety? What were you doing at that moment?
2. Are there specific situations or people that consistently make you feel anxious?
3. Can you recall any past experiences that might be linked to your current anxiety triggers?
4. How does your body react when you're anxious? Do you notice any specific physical sensations?
5. What thoughts run through your mind when you feel anxious? Are there any common themes?

Write down your answers and review them periodically to identify patterns and gain deeper insights into your anxiety triggers.

Mindfulness-based stress reduction (MBSR) exercises can also be beneficial. These exercises help you better understand your thoughts, feelings, and bodily sensations. One effective MBSR exercise is the body scan, where you systematically focus your attention on different parts of your body, noticing any tension or discomfort. This practice can help you become more aware of the physical sensations associated with anxiety, making it easier to identify triggers.

Cognitive-behavioral techniques (CBT) are another valuable tool for identifying anxiety triggers. CBT involves examining the thoughts and beliefs that contribute to your anxiety and challenging them. For instance, if you notice that you feel anxious whenever you think about a particular task at work, you can use CBT techniques to explore and challenge the underlying beliefs that contribute to this anxiety. By identifying and addressing these cognitive patterns, you can reduce the impact of anxiety triggers on your life.

Understanding your anxiety triggers is a vital step in managing anxiety. By becoming more self-aware and analyzing patterns, you can gain valuable insights into what specifically triggers your anxiety. This knowledge empowers you to take proactive steps to manage and reduce anxiety, leading to greater inner peace and well-being.

Mindful Breathing for Anxiety Relief

Mindful breathing is a lifeline in moments of anxiety. Focusing on your breath can bring immediate calm when your heart races and thoughts spiral. It works by activating the parasympathetic nervous system, which counteracts the fight-or-flight response. This shift helps to slow your heart rate, reduce blood pressure, and relax your muscles. The beauty of mindful breathing lies in its simplicity. No matter where you are, you can turn to your breath for relief. I remember a particularly stressful day when I felt overwhelmed by work deadlines. I stepped outside, closed my eyes, and focused on my breath. Within minutes, I felt a wave of calm wash over me, allowing me to return to my tasks with a clearer mind.

Advanced breathing techniques can take your practice to the next level. One such technique is the three-part breath or Dirga

Pranayama. This involves breathing deeply into three parts of your abdomen: first, the lower belly, then the ribcage, and finally, the upper chest. Start by placing one hand on your belly and the other on your chest. Inhale deeply, feel your belly rise, your ribcage expands, and your chest lift. Exhale slowly in reverse order. This technique helps to maximize lung capacity and brings a profound sense of relaxation.

Another powerful technique is the ocean breath, or Ujjayi Pranayama, often used in yoga. To practice, inhale deeply through your nose, then exhale while slightly constricting the back of your throat. This creates a soft, ocean-like sound. The rhythmic nature of this breath can be incredibly soothing, making it an excellent choice for moments of high anxiety.

Resonant or coherent breathing involves inhaling and exhaling for equal lengths, typically around six seconds each. This technique helps to synchronize your breath with your heart rate, promoting a state of calm and balance. It's particularly useful for reducing anxiety and improving overall heart health.

Guided breathing exercises tailored for anxiety relief can be incredibly effective. One approach is to combine breathing with guided imagery. Close your eyes and imagine a peaceful place, like a beach or a forest. As you breathe in, visualize the scenery, and as you breathe out, imagine releasing your anxiety. Another method is to use your breath as an anchor during anxious moments. When you feel anxiety rising, focus solely on your breath. Count each inhale and exhale, aiming for a steady, rhythmic pattern. This can ground you and bring you back to the present moment.

Breath counting is another simple yet powerful exercise for managing anxiety. Sit comfortably and close your eyes. Begin by taking a deep breath in and then slowly exhaling. On the next inhale, silently count "one." On the next exhale, count "two." Continue this pattern up to the count of ten, then start over. This technique can help to focus your mind and reduce anxious thoughts.

Integrating these breathing practices into your daily life can make a significant difference. During high-stress times, take a few minutes to practice mindful breathing. Whether you're in the middle of a hectic workday or dealing with a challenging situation at home, focusing on your breath can provide immediate relief. Incorporating breathing exercises into your morning routine can set a positive tone for the day. Start your morning with a few minutes of deep, mindful breathing to center yourself before diving into your tasks. This can help to reduce stress and improve your focus throughout the day.

Using mindful breathing before social engagements can also be beneficial. If you often feel anxious in social situations, take a few moments to focus on your breath before entering the event. This can help to calm your nerves and make the experience more enjoyable. Practicing mindful breathing regularly can create a sense of inner peace and resilience, making it easier to navigate life's challenges.

Mindful breathing is a simple yet powerful tool for managing anxiety. By incorporating these advanced techniques and guided exercises into your daily routine, you can create moments of calm and clarity, deepening your sense of inner peace.

Grounding Techniques to Stay Present

Grounding techniques are invaluable when it comes to managing anxiety. They are methods that help you stay anchored in the present moment, pulling you out of your anxious thoughts and bringing you back to reality. Think of grounding as a way to tether yourself to the here and now, which can be incredibly calming when anxiety threatens to pull you away. Grounding helps manage anxiety by shifting your focus from the overwhelming feelings in your mind to the tangible sensations in your body. This connection between grounding and mindfulness is important. Both practices encourage you to be present, but grounding is particularly effective in acute anxiety.

Sensory grounding techniques engage your senses—sight, sound, touch, taste, and smell—to bring your mind back to the present. The 5-4-3-2-1 technique is a great place to start. Look around and identify five things you can see, four things you can touch, three things you can hear, two things you can smell, and one thing you can taste. This method can help divert your attention from anxious thoughts to the immediate environment. Touch objects like stress balls or textured items can also be very grounding. The physical sensation of squeezing a stress ball or running your fingers over a textured item can help you focus on something other than your anxiety. Aromatherapy is another effective sensory grounding technique. Scents like lavender, chamomile, or sandalwood can be incredibly soothing. You might find it helpful to carry a small vial of essential oil with you for moments when you need to ground yourself quickly.

Cognitive grounding techniques involve using mental exercises to stay present. Counting backward from 100 is a simple yet effective method. The concentration required to count backward can help distract you from anxious thoughts. Reciting a favorite poem or song lyrics can also be a mental anchor. Familiarity with the words can provide comfort and stability. Mental visualization of a calming place is another powerful cognitive grounding technique. Close your eyes and imagine a place where you feel completely at peace. It could be a beach, a forest, or even a cozy room in your house. Visualize every detail, from the colors and textures to the sounds and smells. This mental escape can provide a much-needed break from anxiety.

Physical grounding techniques involve movement or physical sensations to bring you back to the present. Walking barefoot is a simple yet effective way to ground yourself. Your feet touching the ground can help you feel more connected to your environment.

Progressive muscle relaxation is another excellent physical grounding technique. Start by tensing and then relaxing each muscle group in your body, beginning with your toes and working your way up to your head. This practice can help release physical tension and promote relaxation. Physical exercise with mindful attention, such as yoga or tai chi, can also be incredibly grounding. These practices combine movement with mindfulness, helping you stay present while also benefiting your physical health.

Grounding techniques are versatile and can be adapted to fit into your daily routine. Whether you're at home, at work, or out and about, you can use these methods to manage anxiety and stay present. The key is to find the techniques that work best for you and practice them regularly. Over time, grounding can become a natural and effective way to manage anxiety and maintain a sense of inner peace.

Creating a Calm Space

Your environment plays a significant role in how you feel. Walking into a cluttered room makes it easy to feel overwhelmed and stressed. Clutter can be a constant visual reminder of chaos, making relaxing and finding peace difficult. On the other hand, a calm and organized space can have the opposite effect. It can create a sense of order and tranquility, making it easier to manage anxiety and stress. Imagine walking into a tidy room with soft lighting, soothing colors, and a few well-placed plants. The difference is palpable. Your mind feels at ease, allowing you to breathe a little easier.

Designing a calming space can be done without a complete home makeover. Start with small, intentional changes. Choose soothing colors for your walls and décor. Soft blues, greens, and neutral tones can create a peaceful atmosphere. Avoid bright or harsh colors that can be overstimulating. Incorporating natural elements can also enhance the calming effect. Plants, water features, and natural light can bring a sense of life and serenity to your space. Even a small potted plant on your desk or a water fountain in the corner can make a big difference. Creating dedicated mindfulness areas is another effective strategy. Set aside a corner of your home or office where you can practice mindfulness or simply relax. This could be a cozy chair with a soft blanket, a yoga mat, or even a small altar with items that bring peace.

Mindful organization is about more than just tidying up; it's about creating a space that supports your well-being. Start by decluttering your space. Go through your belongings and decide what you truly need and can let go of. This process can be incredibly liberating. Mindful cleaning practices can also help you maintain a calm space. Instead of rushing through chores, take your time and focus on each task. Notice the smell of the cleaning products, the feel of the cloth in your hand, and the satisfaction of seeing a clean surface. Organizing with intention means placing items in a way that makes sense to you and supports your daily routine. For example, keep your most-used items within easy reach and store less frequently used items out of sight.

Maintaining a calm space requires regular attention. Establishing mindful tidying routines can help you keep your space organized over time. Spend a few minutes daily tidying up rather than letting things pile up. This can prevent clutter from becoming overwhelming. Seasonal reorganization practices can also be helpful. Take some time at the beginning of each season to reassess your space and make any necessary changes. This could include swapping out seasonal décor, reorganizing storage, or deep cleaning certain areas. Setting boundaries to protect your calm space is crucial. Make it clear to others that this space is important for your well-being and should be respected. Whether it's a no-clutter rule or designated quiet times, these boundaries can help maintain the sanctuary you've created.

By creating a calm space, you can significantly reduce your anxiety levels and promote a sense of inner peace. The environment you surround yourself with can either contribute to your stress or help alleviate it. You can create a sanctuary that supports your emotional well-being by making intentional choices and maintaining a mindful organization. This calm space can serve as a refuge from the chaos of daily life, providing a place where you can relax, recharge, and practice mindfulness.

FIVE

Emotional Awareness and Regulation

I remember a particular day when I was overwhelmed with emotions. I had just received some unexpected news at work, and it felt like the ground had been pulled out from under me. My heart raced, my hands trembled, and I couldn't focus on anything else. Later that evening, as I sat quietly reflecting on the day, I realized that an old memory of a similar situation triggered my intense reaction. This moment was a revelation—it made me understand the power of emotional triggers and how they can affect our responses.

Understanding Emotional Triggers

Emotional triggers are specific experiences, memories, or events that spark intense emotional reactions. These reactions can be overwhelming and often seem disproportionate to the situation. For example, a casual comment from a coworker might trigger feelings of rejection, or a particular scent might bring back a flood of memories from a painful period. These triggers are deeply personal and can vary widely from one person to another. Common sources of emotional triggers include past experiences, relationships, and even unconscious biases that we've developed over time.

Past experiences play a significant role in shaping our emotional triggers. For instance, if you experienced betrayal in a past relationship, you might feel anxious or distrustful in new relationships, even when there's no immediate reason for concern. Past and present relationships are also fertile ground for emotional triggers. A critical comment from a partner or a perceived slight from a friend can bring up deep-seated feelings of inadequacy or rejection. Unconscious biases can trigger emotional responses, too. These biases often form in childhood and can affect how we perceive and react to certain situations.

Reflecting on your emotional triggers is the first step toward understanding and managing them. Journaling can be an incredibly effective tool for this. Set aside time each day to write about your experiences and emotions. When did you feel particularly upset or anxious? What was happening at that moment? By regularly journaling, you can identify patterns and pinpoint specific triggers. Mindful reflection exercises can also be beneficial. Take a few minutes each day to sit quietly and reflect on your emotional responses. What thoughts and feelings arise when you think about certain situations or people? This practice can help you become more aware of your triggers and how they affect you.

Identifying patterns in your emotional responses is crucial. Over time, certain situations consistently trigger strong reactions. For example, you might feel particularly anxious during work team meetings or become defensive whenever someone criticizes your work. Recognizing these patterns can help you anticipate and manage your triggers more effectively.

Emotional triggers can have a profound impact on our behavior and decision-making. When triggered, we might react in ways that are out of character or that we later regret. For example, you might avoid social situations because they trigger insecurity or lash out in anger when you feel disrespected. These behaviors are often automatic responses to the underlying emotional trigger. The connection between triggers and stress responses is well-documented. When triggered, our bodies become heightened alert, activating the fight-or-flight response. This can lead to physical symptoms like a pounding heart, sweaty palms, or an upset stomach.

Managing Emotional Triggers

Case studies can illustrate the impact of emotional triggers. Take Allie, for example. She experienced intense anxiety whenever she received feedback at work. Through journaling and therapy, she realized that this anxiety was linked to her childhood experiences of being harshly criticized by a parent. By understanding this connection, Allie was able to develop healthier coping mechanisms and reduce her anxiety during feedback sessions.

Managing emotional triggers involves both short-term and long-term strategies. Mindfulness techniques can be incredibly effective for early detection of triggers. When you notice a strong emotional response, take a moment to pause and breathe. Use mindful breathing to ground yourself and create a space between the trigger and your reaction. Developing healthy coping mechanisms is also crucial. This might involve talking to a trusted friend, practicing self-compassion, or engaging in activities that help you relax and recharge.

Creating a trigger action plan can provide a structured approach to managing your triggers. Start by identifying your most common triggers and the situations in which they occur. Next, outline specific strategies for managing these triggers when they arise. For example, if social situations trigger anxiety, your action plan might include practicing deep breathing exercises before attending an event and setting a time limit for how long you'll stay. Having a plan can help you feel more prepared and in control.

Reflection Exercise: Exploring Emotional Triggers

Take a few moments to reflect on your emotional triggers. Consider the following questions and write down your thoughts:

1. What situations or experiences consistently evoke strong emotional reactions in you?
2. Can you trace these reactions back to past experiences or relationships?
3. How do these emotional triggers affect your behavior and decision-making?
4. What physical symptoms do you notice when you're triggered?
5. What strategies have you found helpful in managing your emotional triggers?

Understanding and managing your emotional triggers allows you to navigate life's challenges with greater ease and resilience. This awareness allows you to respond to situations thoughtfully rather than impulsively, creating a deeper sense of inner peace and emotional balance.

Mindful Observation of Emotions

The Practice of Observing Emotions means tuning into your feelings without trying to change or judge them. It's about noticing the waves of emotion that pass through you, allowing them to exist without immediately reacting. Observing emotions mindfully involves separating the emotion from your reaction to it. For example, if you feel anger rising, instead of lashing out or suppressing it, you simply acknowledge its presence. This practice can be incredibly liberating. It allows you to understand your emotional landscape better and respond more thoughtfully. The benefits are numerous. Mindful observation can reduce the intensity of negative emotions, improve emotional regulation, and create a sense of inner peace.

To practice mindful observation, start with a body scan to notice emotional sensations. Find a quiet place to sit or lie down, close your eyes, and take a few deep breaths. Begin by focusing on your toes and slowly move your attention up through your body, noticing any areas of tension or discomfort. As you do this, pay attention to any emotional sensations that arise. For instance, you might notice a tightness in your chest that corresponds with anxiety or a heaviness in your shoulders that signals stress. This body scan can help you become more aware of the physical manifestations of your emotions.

Another effective technique is labeling your emotions without judgment. When you notice an emotion, simply give it a name. "This is anger," or "This is sadness." By labeling the emotion, you create a space between yourself and the feeling, which can make it less overwhelming. It's like stepping back and observing a storm from a safe distance rather than being caught in the middle. This practice can help you understand your emotions better and respond more calmly.

Using your breath as an anchor during emotional waves is another powerful tool. When you feel a strong emotion coming on, focus on your breath. Take slow, deep breaths, and pay attention to the sensation of air entering and leaving your body. This can help ground you and keep you present, preventing the emotion from taking over. Imagine your breath as a steady anchor that holds you in place while the emotional storm passes. This technique can be particularly useful in moments of intense emotion, providing a simple yet effective way to stay centered.

Staying present with difficult emotions without becoming overwhelmed is a skill that takes practice. One technique is grounding yourself during intense emotions. This can involve focusing on your senses to return to the present moment. For example, you might press your feet firmly into the ground, hold a textured object, or focus on the sounds around you. These grounding techniques can help you stay present and prevent the emotion from spiraling out of control.

Practicing self-compassion during emotional observation is also crucial. When you notice a difficult emotion, offer yourself kindness and understanding. Remind yourself that it's okay to feel this way and that it's a natural part of being human. This self-compassion can create a sense of safety and support, making staying present with the emotion easier. Recognizing the transient nature of emotions can also be incredibly helpful. Emotions are like waves—they rise, peak, and eventually fade. Remind yourself that this difficult emotion, too, will pass. This awareness can make the emotion feel less permanent and more manageable.

Reflective practices can deepen your emotional awareness. A daily emotion log is a great way to track your emotional experiences. Each day, take a few minutes to write down your emotions, what triggered them, and how you responded. This practice can help you identify patterns and gain deeper insights into your emotional landscape. Guided mindful journaling exercises can also be beneficial. Set aside time each day to journal about your emotions, using prompts to guide your reflection. For example, you might write about a recent emotional experience and explore how you felt, what triggered it, and how you responded. This reflective practice can help you understand your emotions better and develop healthier ways to manage them.

Personal stories of transformation through mindful observation can be inspiring. Take Emily, for example. She struggled with intense bouts of anger that would often lead to arguments with her partner. Through mindful observation, she learned to notice the early signs of anger, such as a tightening in her chest and rapid breathing. Labeling the emotion and using her breath as an anchor, she could stay present and choose a more thoughtful response. This practice transformed her relationship, reducing conflicts and creating a deeper connection.

Mindful observation of emotions is a powerful practice that can help you better understand and manage your emotional landscape. By observing your emotions mindfully, you can create a sense of inner peace and emotional balance. This practice allows you to respond to emotions thoughtfully rather than reacting impulsively, leading to healthier and more fulfilling relationships.

Techniques for Emotional Regulation

Emotional regulation is the ability to manage and respond to emotional experiences healthily. It's not about suppressing your emotions or pretending they don't exist. Instead, it's about understanding your emotions, accepting them, and finding constructive ways to cope with them. This skill is crucial for mental well-being because it helps you navigate life's ups and downs without becoming overwhelmed. When you can regulate your emotions, you're better equipped to handle stress, maintain healthy relationships, and make thoughtful decisions.

One common misconception is that emotional regulation means pushing your emotions aside. This couldn't be further from the truth. Suppression involves ignoring or denying your feelings, which can lead to increased stress and emotional outbursts later on. Emotional regulation, on the other hand, involves acknowledging your emotions and dealing with them in a healthy and constructive way. For instance, if you feel angry, instead of bottling it up, you might take a few deep breaths, acknowledge your anger, and find a healthy outlet for it, like talking to a friend or walking.

The role of emotional regulation in stress management cannot be overstated. When you can regulate your emotions, you're less likely to feel overwhelmed by stress. You can approach stressful situations with a clear mind and a calm demeanor, making it easier to find solutions and navigate challenges. This skill is particularly important for managing anxiety and perfectionism, as it helps you maintain balance and perspective.

Mindfulness-based techniques are incredibly effective for emotional regulation. One popular method is the RAIN technique, which stands for Recognize, Allow, Investigate, and Nurture. When you experience a strong emotion, start by recognizing it. Name the emotion and acknowledge its presence. Next, allow the emotion to be there without trying to change it. Investigate the emotion with curiosity, exploring its origins and how it feels in your body. Finally, nurture yourself with kindness and compassion, offering yourself the understanding and support you need.

Another useful practice is the S.T.O.P. technique: Stop, Take a breath, Observe, Proceed. When you feel overwhelmed, pause and take a deep breath. Observe what's happening inside you and around you. What thoughts are running through your mind? What physical sensations are you experiencing? Then, proceed with a mindful response instead of a knee-jerk reaction. This simple technique can create a space between your emotion and reaction, allowing you to choose a more thoughtful response.

The emotion surfboard method is another valuable tool. Imagine your emotions as waves in the ocean. Some waves are small and gentle, while others are large and powerful. Instead of fighting the waves or getting swept away, picture yourself riding them on a surfboard. Stay balanced and ride each wave as it comes, knowing it will eventually pass. This visualization can help you remain steady and calm amidst emotional turbulence.

Cognitive-behavioral approaches complement mindfulness practices and offer additional tools for emotional regulation. Cognitive restructuring, for example, involves identifying and challenging negative thought patterns. When you notice a negative thought, ask yourself if it's based on facts or assumptions. Then, reframe the thought in a more balanced and realistic way. This can help shift your perspective and reduce the emotional impact of negative thinking.

Thought-stopping techniques are also effective. When contemplating or spiraling into negative thoughts, use a mental cue to interrupt the pattern. You might say "stop" to yourself or visualize a stop sign. Then, redirect your focus to something positive or neutral. This practice can help break the cycle of negative thinking and prevent it from escalating.

Reframing negative thoughts is another powerful strategy. Instead of seeing a situation as entirely negative, look for the silver lining or a different perspective. For example, if you make a mistake at work, instead of beating yourself up, consider what you can learn from the experience. This shift in perspective can reduce the emotional weight of negative experiences and promote a more positive outlook.

Creating an emotional regulation plan can provide a structured approach to managing emotions. Start by identifying your triggers and typical responses. What situations or experiences tend to evoke strong emotions? How do you usually react? Once you clearly understand your triggers and responses, develop a step-by-step regulation strategy. This might include mindfulness practices, cognitive-behavioral techniques, and healthy coping mechanisms. Incorporate these practices into your daily routine to build emotional resilience and improve your ability to regulate emotions.

By understanding and employing these techniques, you can develop a robust emotional regulation plan that supports your mental well-being. Emotional regulation is a skill that can be cultivated with practice and patience, leading to a deeper sense of inner peace and balance.

Building Emotional Resilience

Emotional resilience is the ability to bounce back from life's challenges and setbacks. It's about maintaining a stable emotional state even when things go wrong. Emotional resilience isn't about never experiencing negative emotions but rather about how quickly and effectively you can recover from them. The benefits of emotional resilience are profound. Resilient individuals tend to have better mental health, stronger relationships, and greater overall well-being. They are more adaptable, can handle stress better, and are often more optimistic about the future.

Imagine a storm hitting a tree. A resilient tree bends with the wind but doesn't break. Similarly, resilient individuals can endure stress and adversity without crumbling. They find ways to cope, adapt, and eventually thrive even in the face of challenges. This resilience is closely linked to overall well-being because it enables you to navigate life's ups and downs with balance and stability. Examples of resilient behaviors include seeking support when needed, maintaining a positive outlook, and using setbacks as opportunities for growth.

Mindfulness practices can play a crucial role in building emotional resilience. Loving-kindness meditation is one such practice. This involves directing feelings of love and compassion towards yourself and others. By regularly practicing loving-kindness meditation, you can cultivate a sense of warmth and connection, which can bolster your emotional resilience. Gratitude journaling is another powerful tool. Each day, take a few minutes to write down things you're grateful for. This practice can shift your focus from what's going wrong to what's going right, fostering a more positive outlook and enhancing resilience.

Mindful self-reflection is also essential. Set aside time each day to reflect on your experiences and emotions. This can help you gain insights into your emotional responses and develop healthier coping methods. Regularly engaging in mindful self-reflection can build a deeper understanding of yourself and strengthen your emotional resilience.

Cultivating a growth mindset is another key factor in developing emotional resilience. A growth mindset is the belief that you can develop your abilities and intelligence through effort and learning. This contrasts with a fixed mindset, which holds that your abilities are static and unchangeable. By adopting a growth mindset, you can view challenges as opportunities for growth rather than threats. Techniques for fostering a growth mindset include embracing challenges, learning from criticism, and persisting in the face of setbacks.

Case studies illustrate the power of a growth mindset in building resilience. Take the example of Amanda, who faced significant setbacks in her career. Instead of viewing these setbacks as failures, she saw them as opportunities to learn and grow. By adopting a growth mindset, Amanda could bounce back stronger, eventually achieving even greater success. Her resilience was about enduring the challenges and using them as stepping stones for personal and professional growth.

Social support is another crucial element in building emotional resilience. Identifying supportive relationships can provide a safety net during tough times. These relationships might include friends, family members, colleagues, or support groups. Techniques for seeking and offering support involve open communication, active listening, and being present for others. Creating a community of resilience means surrounding yourself with people who understand and support your journey.

Building a support network can significantly enhance your resilience. For instance, joining a mindfulness group can provide a sense of community and shared experience. These groups offer a safe space to share your struggles and successes, providing emotional support and practical advice. Similarly, cultivating strong relationships with friends and family can provide comfort and encouragement during difficult times.

Focusing on these practices and principles can help you build emotional resilience and navigate life's challenges with greater ease and confidence. Emotional resilience is not a trait you're born with but a skill you can develop through mindful practices, a growth mindset, and a strong support network. This resilience will be a foundation for your well-being, helping you maintain balance and find peace amidst life's inevitable storms.

Next, we'll explore how to integrate mindfulness into everyday activities, making it a seamless part of your life. This will help you maintain the emotional resilience you've built and continue to grow in your journey toward inner peace.

SIX

Overcoming Negative Self-Talk

One day, I was getting ready for a big presentation at work. I stood in front of the mirror, rehearsing my lines, but all I could hear was that nagging voice in my head saying, "You're going to mess this up. Everyone will see how incompetent you are." My chest tightened, and I felt a wave of panic. It was at that moment I realized how powerful negative self-talk could be and how it had been undermining my confidence for years. I knew it was time to address these harmful thoughts head-on.

Recognizing Negative Thought Patterns

Negative self-talk refers to the critical, negative, or punishing internal comments about ourselves. These thoughts can be incredibly damaging, influencing our mental health and self-image. When you constantly hear a voice in your head telling you that you're not good enough, it's hard not to believe it. This internal dialogue can keep you stuck in a cycle of self-doubt and anxiety, making it challenging to move forward and achieve your goals.

Negative self-talk comes in various forms. One common type is catastrophizing, where you imagine the worst possible outcome in any situation. For instance, if you make a small mistake at work, you might think, "I'm going to get fired for this." Another type is overgeneralizing, where you see a single negative event as a never-ending pattern of defeat. For example, if you fail a test, you might think, "I always fail at everything." These thoughts can erode your self-esteem and mental well-being, leaving you feeling hopeless and defeated.

The impact of negative self-talk on self-esteem and mental well-being is profound. Constantly berating yourself can lead to feelings of worthlessness and depression. It can also increase your anxiety, as you're always anticipating failure or rejection. Over time, this negative internal dialogue can become a self-fulfilling prophecy. When you believe you're not good enough, you may stop trying, reinforcing the very failures you fear.

Common negative thought patterns include all-or-nothing thinking, where you see things in black-and-white terms. If something isn't perfect, it's a complete failure. Mental filtering is another pattern where you focus on the negative aspects of a situation and ignore the positive. For example, you might receive a glowing performance review but fixate on one constructive criticism. Disqualifying the positive involves rejecting positive experiences by insisting they "don't count." You might think, "Sure, I got a promotion, but it's just because no one else wanted the job." Jumping to conclusions is another pattern, where you make negative assumptions without evidence. For instance, you might assume someone is mad at you even though they haven't said anything to suggest that.

Self-monitoring techniques can help you become aware of your negative thought patterns. Keeping a thought diary is an effective method. Write down your thoughts throughout the day, especially when you notice a shift in your mood. Note what you were doing and how you felt. This can help you identify recurring patterns and specific triggers for your negative self-talk. Mindfulness meditation is another powerful tool. Practicing mindfulness lets you observe your thoughts without getting caught up in them. This awareness can help you recognize negative self-talk as it happens, allowing you to challenge and change it.

Using phone apps to track negative thoughts can also be helpful. Apps like Thought Diary or CBT Thought Record Diary can assist you in recording and analyzing your thoughts. These apps often include prompts and exercises to help you reframe negative thoughts and develop a more balanced perspective. The convenience of having these tools on your phone makes it easier to integrate self-monitoring into your daily routine.

Understanding the triggers for your negative self-talk is crucial. Reflecting on past experiences can provide valuable insights. Think about situations where you felt particularly down on yourself. What was happening at the time? Were you under a lot of stress? Did someone say something that made you doubt yourself? Identifying specific triggers, such as stressful work situations or social interactions, can help you anticipate and manage your negative self-talk.

Using mindfulness to notice immediate reactions can also be beneficial. Pay attention to how your body feels when you're experiencing negative self-talk. Do you feel tension in your shoulders? Is your heart racing? These physical sensations can serve as cues to check in with your thoughts. When you notice these reactions, take a moment to breathe deeply and observe your thoughts without judgment. This can help you interrupt the cycle of negative self-talk and create space for more positive, constructive thoughts.

Reflection Exercise: Identifying Negative Thought Patterns

Take a moment to reflect on your recent thoughts. Write down any negative thoughts you've had in the past week. Note the context and how you felt at the time. Look for patterns and triggers. Are there specific situations that tend to bring out your negative self-talk? How do these thoughts impact your mood and behavior? This exercise can help you become more aware of your thought patterns and provide a starting point for changing them.

Recognizing and understanding your negative thought patterns is the first step towards overcoming them. By becoming aware of these patterns and their triggers, you can start challenging and changing your negative self-talk, paving the way for a more positive and balanced mindset.

Transforming Negative Thoughts

Cognitive restructuring is a powerful method to challenge and change negative thought patterns. This therapeutic technique involves deconstructing unhelpful thoughts and rebuilding them in a balanced and accurate way. Imagine you're wearing a pair of dark glasses that distort your vision; cognitive restructuring helps you swap those for clearer lenses. The process begins with identifying a negative thought. Once pinpointing the thought, ask yourself if it's based on facts or assumptions. Often, our negative thoughts are not grounded in reality. Next, challenge the thought by considering alternative perspectives. For example, if you think, "I always mess up," ask yourself if that's entirely true. Have there been times when you succeeded? Finally, replace the negative thought with a more balanced one, like, "I've made mistakes, but I've also had successes."

Positive reframing is another effective technique for transforming negative thoughts into positive or neutral ones. This involves shifting your perspective to see the situation in a different light. For instance, if you're thinking, "I failed at this project," you can reframe it to, "This project didn't go as planned, but it's an opportunity to learn and improve." Techniques for positive reframing include asking yourself what you can learn from the experience, how you might grow from it, and how you would advise a friend in the same situation. Real-life scenarios show the power of positive reframing. Take Sarah, who was upset about a job rejection. Instead of dwelling on the rejection, she reframed it as a chance to find a better fit for her skills and values. This shift in perspective helped her stay motivated and eventually land a job that was a perfect match.

Mindful self-compassion techniques can also counteract negative self-talk. Loving-kindness meditation focused on self is a powerful practice. Sit comfortably, close your eyes, and bring a sense of warmth and compassion to your mind. Repeat phrases like, "May I be happy. May I be healthy. May I be safe. May I live with ease." This practice helps cultivate a sense of kindness towards yourself, reducing the harshness of negative self-talk. Self-compassion breaks are another useful tool. When you notice negative self-talk, pause and acknowledge it. Say to yourself, "This is a moment of suffering. Suffering is a part of life. May I be kind to myself." This simple practice can shift your mindset from self-criticism to self-compassion, fostering self-acceptance and emotional resilience.

Exercises for fostering self-acceptance can further enhance your ability to counteract negative self-talk. One effective exercise is to write a letter to yourself from the perspective of a compassionate friend. In this letter, acknowledge your struggles and offer words of kindness and encouragement. This practice can help you see yourself through a kinder lens, reducing the impact of negative self-talk. Another exercise is to practice mirror work. Stand before a mirror, look into your eyes, and say kind words to yourself. This can initially feel awkward, but it's a powerful way to build self-acceptance and counteract negative thoughts.

Daily affirmation practice is another powerful tool for replacing negative thoughts with positive ones. Creating personalized affirmations involves identifying areas where you struggle with negative self-talk and crafting positive statements to counteract those thoughts. For example, if you often think, "I'm not good enough," you can create an affirmation like, "I am worthy and capable." Practical tips for daily affirmation practice include writing your affirmations on sticky notes and placing them where you'll see them often, such as on your bathroom mirror or computer screen. You can also set reminders on your phone to repeat your affirmations throughout the day.

Success stories from individuals using affirmations highlight their transformative power. Take Emily, who struggled with self-doubt. She began using affirmations like, "I am confident and strong," and repeated them every morning and evening. Over time, she noticed a shift in her mindset. She felt more confident and less plagued by negative self-talk. Another example is Lisa, who used affirmations to combat feelings of inadequacy at work. By repeating affirmations like, "I am capable and competent," she gradually built her self-esteem and improved her performance.

Transforming negative thoughts takes practice and patience. Cognitive restructuring, positive reframing, mindful self-compassion techniques, and daily affirmations are powerful tools that can help you shift your mindset and cultivate a more positive and balanced outlook.

Affirmations for Self-Love

Imagine waking up each morning to a voice that says, "You are capable, you are strong, and today is your day." This is the power of affirmations. Research supports the effectiveness of affirmations in transforming self-talk. Repeated positive statements can rewire your brain, shifting your mindset from negativity to empowerment. Studies have shown that affirmations can increase neural pathways associated with self-worth and resilience. For example, athletes who use affirmations often perform better because they believe in their abilities. Similarly, individuals who consistently practice positive affirmations report higher self-esteem and mental well-being levels.

Creating effective affirmations requires a bit of thought, but it's well worth the effort. The most powerful affirmations are specific, positive, and in the present tense. Rather than saying, "I will be happy," say, "I am happy." This phrasing helps your mind accept the statement as truth. Personalizing your affirmations is crucial. Think about areas where you struggle with self-love and craft affirmations that speak directly to those issues. For example, if you struggle with feeling worthy, an affirmation like, "I am deserving of love and respect," can be incredibly powerful. Other areas to consider could be confidence, self-acceptance, and resilience. Affirmations like "I trust myself" or "I am enough just as I am" can target these aspects effectively.

Incorporating affirmations into your daily routine can make a significant difference. Start your day with a morning affirmation ritual. As soon as you wake up, take a moment to say your affirmations out loud. This sets a positive tone for the day. Similarly, end your day with evening affirmations to reflect on your accomplishments and reinforce positive self-talk. Using affirmation apps can also be helpful. These apps can send you reminders throughout the day, prompting you to take a moment for positive self-talk. Writing affirmations in visible places is another practical approach. Sticky notes on your mirror, affirmations in your journal, or even setting them as your phone wallpaper can constantly remind you of your worth and capabilities.

Affirmation Exercises: Practicing and Internalizing Affirmations

One effective exercise is affirmation journaling. Write down your affirmations each day and reflect on how they make you feel. Notice any shifts in your mindset or mood. This practice reinforces your positive statements and helps you internalize them. Another powerful exercise is mirror work. Stand in front of a mirror, look into your own eyes, and say your affirmations out loud. This can be challenging at first, but it's incredibly impactful. Looking at yourself while speaking kindness can help break down barriers of self-doubt and build a stronger sense of self-love.

Recording and listening to your affirmations can also be beneficial. Use your phone or a recording device to capture yourself saying your affirmations. Play these recordings during your morning routine, commuting, or before bed. Hearing your voice affirming your worth can amplify the positive impact, making the affirmations feel more genuine and powerful.

Affirmations are not just words; they are powerful tools that can transform your self-talk and boost your self-love. Integrating these practices into your daily life can create a foundation of positivity and resilience, helping you manage anxiety, control, and perfectionism with grace and confidence.

Journaling for Positive Self-Talk

One evening, after a particularly tough day, I found solace in an old notebook. I began writing about my frustrations, my fears, and everything that had been weighing me down. As the pen moved across the paper, something shifted. The chaos in my mind started to clear, and I felt a sense of relief. This was my introduction to the transformative power of journaling.

Journaling offers numerous psychological benefits. Expressive writing helps process emotions, providing a safe space to explore thoughts and feelings. It serves as an emotional release, allowing you to let go of stress and anxiety. Case studies show that individuals who journal regularly experience improved mental clarity and emotional well-being. Take, for instance, Courtney, who struggled with anxiety.

She began journaling daily, and over time, she noticed a significant reduction in her anxiety levels. The act of writing helped her identify triggers and develop healthier coping mechanisms.

There are various journaling techniques specifically aimed at fostering positive self-talk. Gratitude journaling is a powerful practice. Each day, write down three things you're grateful for. This simple act shifts your focus from what's wrong to what's right, fostering a positive mindset. Reflective journaling involves writing about your thoughts and experiences, helping you gain insights and learn from them. This technique encourages self-reflection and growth. Prompt-based journaling is another effective method. You can explore specific aspects of your life and thoughts using guided prompts, facilitating deeper self-awareness and positive self-talk.

Guided journal prompts can help you focus on positive aspects of yourself and your life. Prompts for self-reflection and growth might include questions like, "What have I learned from a recent challenge?" or "How have I grown in the past year?" These questions encourage you to reflect on your progress and achievements. Affirmation-based journal prompts can help reinforce positive self-talk. Write about affirmations you believe in, such as "I am capable of achieving my goals," and reflect on how they make you feel. Prompts for recognizing personal strengths and achievements might include, "What are three things I'm proud of?" or "What strengths have helped me overcome challenges?" These prompts help you acknowledge and celebrate your qualities and accomplishments.

Creating a consistent journaling routine is key to reaping the benefits of this practice. Set aside dedicated journaling time each day. It could be in the morning to set a positive tone for the day or in the evening to reflect on your experiences. Creating a conducive journaling environment can also enhance the experience. Find a quiet, comfortable space where you can write without distractions. Light a candle or play soft music to create a calming atmosphere. Techniques for overcoming writer's block include starting with a simple prompt or free-writing for a few minutes. Remember, there's no right or wrong way to journal. The goal is to express yourself freely and authentically.

Journaling can be a powerful tool for positive self-talk, offering a space to process emotions, reflect on experiences, and celebrate achievements. Integrating journaling into your daily routine can cultivate a positive mindset and enhance your emotional well-being.

In the next chapter, we'll explore practical mindfulness techniques for managing stress and fostering a deeper sense of inner peace.

SEVEN

Balancing Multiple Roles with Mindfulness

I remember a particular morning when I was juggling multiple roles—professional deadlines, family commitments, and personal aspirations. My to-do list felt like a never-ending scroll, and I was drowning in tasks. Then, I realized I needed a different approach to managing my time and responsibilities effectively. This is where mindful time management came into play, transforming my chaotic days into more balanced and fulfilling ones.

Mindful Time Management

Mindfulness can significantly enhance your ability to identify and prioritize tasks effectively. Getting caught up in the whirlwind of daily activities is easy, but mindfulness encourages you to pause and reflect on what truly matters. By paying attention to your life moment by moment, you can make conscious decisions about how to spend your time, committing to what is most important to you. Techniques for mindful prioritization include starting your day with a few minutes of meditation to clear your mind and set your intentions. This practice helps you focus on tasks that align with your values and goals rather than getting sidetracked by less important activities.

Creating a mindful to-do list is another powerful tool. Instead of listing everything you need to do, prioritize tasks by their importance and urgency. Use categories like "Must Do," "Should Do," and "Could Do" to organize your list. This method helps you focus on high-priority tasks first, reducing the overwhelm of a long to-do list. Tools like digital planners or mindfulness apps can assist in creating and managing these lists efficiently. For example, apps like Todoist or Trello allow you to categorize and prioritize tasks, making it easier to stay on track.

Case studies of effective prioritization highlight the benefits of these techniques. Take Mariah, a busy marketing manager and mother of two. By incorporating mindful prioritization into her routine, she could identify and focus on her most important tasks at work and home. She started her day with a brief meditation, listing her top three priorities for the day. This approach helped her stay focused and productive while making time for her family and self-care.

Mindful scheduling is about creating a balanced schedule that allows you to manage your work, family, and personal time effectively. One tip is to block out time for mindfulness practices. Set aside specific times during the day for meditation, deep breathing, or mindful walking. These breaks help you recharge and maintain your focus throughout the day. Examples of balanced daily schedules include a morning routine with meditation, a midday break for a mindful walk, and an evening wind-down with a body scan meditation.

Avoiding over-scheduling is crucial for maintaining balance. It's tempting to fill every minute of your day with tasks, but this can lead to burnout. Instead, leave some buffer time between tasks to allow for unexpected events or simply to take a breather. Strategies for avoiding over-scheduling include setting realistic goals and learning to say no to additional commitments that don't align with your priorities.

Staying present with tasks is essential for reducing stress and increasing productivity. When you focus on one task at a time, you can complete it more efficiently and effectively. Mindful task-switching involves taking a moment to pause and breathe before moving from one task to another. This practice helps you reset and approach each new task with a clear and focused mind. Techniques for minimizing distractions include turning off notifications, setting specific times for checking emails and creating a designated workspace free from interruptions.

Real-life examples of improved focus demonstrate the power of staying present with tasks. Consider Kelsey, a freelance writer struggling to stay focused due to constant distractions. By practicing mindful task-switching and minimizing distractions, she improved her concentration and completed her projects more efficiently. She turned off her phone notifications and set specific times for checking emails, allowing her to stay immersed in her writing.

Reflective time management encourages regular reflection on your time use to make mindful adjustments as needed. Weekly time management reflections help you assess how well you balance your responsibilities and identify areas for improvement. Set aside a few minutes each week to review your schedule and reflect on what worked and what didn't. This practice allows you to make adjustments and realign your priorities.

Journaling prompts for assessing time use can guide your reflections. Questions like "What tasks brought me the most satisfaction this week?" and "Were there any activities that felt like a waste of time?" can help you gain insights into how you spend your time. Techniques for realigning priorities include adjusting your to-do list, setting new goals, and making deliberate choices about where to focus your energy.

By incorporating mindful time management practices into your routine, you can more effectively balance your multiple roles, reduce stress, and create a sense of inner peace.

Setting Boundaries with Mindfulness

Understanding personal boundaries is crucial for mental well-being. Personal boundaries are the limits and rules we set for ourselves within relationships, defining what we are comfortable with and how we wish to be treated. These boundaries can be emotional, physical, or related to time. Emotional boundaries involve protecting your feelings and mental health, ensuring that others do not manipulate or emotionally drain you. Physical boundaries pertain to your personal space and physical touch. Time boundaries involve managing how you spend your time and energy, ensuring you have time for yourself and your priorities. Establishing and maintaining these boundaries can significantly reduce stress and help you manage anxiety and control.

Mindful boundary setting involves being aware of your needs and communicating them clearly and compassionately. Start by identifying what your boundaries are. This requires self-reflection and mindfulness to understand what makes you uncomfortable or stressed. Techniques for identifying boundary needs include journaling about situations where you felt overwhelmed or taken advantage of and noting your physical and emotional reactions. Once you clearly understand your boundaries, the next step is mindful communication. This means expressing your boundaries in a calm and respectful manner. For example, if you need some alone time after work to unwind, you might say, "I need some quiet time for myself after work to relax. I'll join you for dinner afterward." This approach ensures your needs are met without causing unnecessary conflict.

Examples of healthy boundaries in action can be incredibly inspiring. Take, for instance, a friend who struggled with work-life balance. She realized she needed to set clear boundaries with her boss about after-hours communication. After some reflection, she decided to talk with her boss, explaining that she would not be available for work-related calls or emails after 7 PM. This boundary allowed her to spend quality time with her family and reduced her stress levels significantly. Another example is a colleague who set boundaries with a friend who often vented about personal problems, leaving her emotionally drained. She compassionately communicated her need for space and proposed setting specific times for their chats, ensuring she could provide support without feeling overwhelmed.

Saying no mindfully and compassionately is an art that requires practice. Many of us struggle with saying no because we fear disappointing others or facing conflict. However, it's possible to refuse requests with kindness and without guilt. Scripts for compassionate refusal can be helpful. For example, suppose a colleague asks you to take on an extra project, and you're already overwhelmed. In that case, you might say, "I appreciate you thinking of me for this project, but I'm currently at capacity with my workload. I won't be able to give it the attention it deserves." This response is respectful and considerate while firmly setting your boundaries. Techniques for handling pushback include staying calm, reiterating your boundaries, and offering alternatives if possible. For instance, "I understand this project is important, but I can't take it on now. Perhaps we can revisit it next month, or I can help you find someone else to assist."

Personal stories of assertive boundary setting can provide valuable insights and encouragement. A close friend of mine used to feel obligated to attend every family gathering, even when it exhausted her. She set boundaries around these events after practicing mindfulness and reflecting on her needs. She told her family that she would attend major celebrations but needed downtime on other weekends. Although initially challenging, her family eventually respected her boundaries, and she felt more balanced and less stressed.

Maintaining boundaries consistently over time is crucial for their effectiveness. Regular boundary check-ins help ensure your boundaries are still serving you well. Set aside time to reflect on your boundaries and whether they need adjustment. Mindfulness practices for reinforcing boundaries include meditation and self-reflection exercises that help you stay connected to your needs. Techniques for adjusting boundaries as needed involve being flexible and open to change. Life circumstances can evolve, and your boundaries may need to shift accordingly. For example, you may need to tighten your boundaries during particularly stressful periods or relax when you have more capacity.

Incorporating these mindful practices into your life can help you establish and maintain healthy boundaries, reduce stress, and enhance your overall well-being. By being clear about your needs and communicating them compassionately, you can create a balanced and fulfilling life.

Mindful Parenting Techniques

I remember the moment vividly. My toddler was having a full-blown meltdown in the middle of the grocery store, and I felt all eyes on me. My stress levels were through the roof. At that moment, I took a deep breath and tried something new: mindfulness. I focused on my breath, grounded myself, and responded to my child calmly and empathetically. At that moment, I changed my approach to parenting forever.

Mindfulness can profoundly enhance your parenting skills and improve parent-child relationships. The benefits of mindful parenting are numerous. Being fully present with your children can foster deeper connections, improve communication, and create a more peaceful home environment. Mindfulness helps you respond to your child's needs with patience and understanding rather than reacting out of frustration or stress. Real-life examples abound. Consider a mother who practices mindfulness during her morning routine with her kids. Instead of rushing through breakfast, she takes time to engage with them, listen to their stories, and share their excitement for the day. This simple practice sets a positive tone for the family and strengthens their bond.

One of the key elements of mindful parenting is mindful communication with your children. Active listening exercises can help you truly hear and understand your child's thoughts and feelings. When your child speaks, focus entirely on them. Make eye contact, nod in acknowledgment, and refrain from interrupting. This practice shows your child that their voice matters and builds trust. Techniques for empathetic responses are equally important. Reflect on what your child has said to show understanding. For instance, if your child says, "I'm scared of the dark," you might respond, "It sounds like the dark makes you feel uncomfortable. What can we do to help you feel better?" Scripts for mindful conversations can guide you through challenging discussions. When addressing a conflict, use "I" statements to express your feelings and needs without blaming them. For example, "I feel worried when you don't finish your homework because I want you to succeed. How can we work together to make sure it gets done?"

Parenting is inherently stressful, but mindfulness practices can help manage these challenges. Mindful breathing exercises for parents offer a quick way to calm your mind and body. Take a few deep breaths, focusing on the sensation of air entering and leaving your lungs. This simple practice can reduce stress and help you respond to your child's needs with greater patience. Techniques for staying calm during tantrums are invaluable. When your child is in a meltdown, try grounding yourself by feeling the floor beneath your feet and taking slow, deep breaths. This can help you maintain your composure and handle the situation more effectively. Self-compassion practices for parenting guilt are also crucial. It's easy to feel guilty when you don't meet your high standards as a parent. Remind yourself that it's okay to be imperfect. Offer yourself the same kindness and understanding you would extend to a friend in a similar situation.

Creating mindful family practices can further enhance your parenting and family dynamics. Family mindfulness meditation sessions can be a wonderful way to bond and cultivate a sense of calm together. Choose a quiet time before bed, and guide your family through a short meditation. Focus on the breath, body sensations, or a calming visualization. This practice can help everyone unwind and connect on a deeper level. Mindful eating as a family is another great practice. During meals, encourage everyone to pay attention to the food's flavors, textures, and smells. Share what you appreciate about the meal and express gratitude for the nourishment. This can transform mealtime into a mindful and enjoyable family ritual. A family mindfulness corner can provide a dedicated space for these practices. Choose a cozy spot in your home, add some cushions, calming decorations, and perhaps a few mindfulness tools like a singing bowl or essential oils. This space can serve as a sanctuary for family members to retreat to when they need a moment of calm.

Mindful parenting is not about being a perfect parent. It's about being present, compassionate, and responsive to your child's needs. Incorporating these mindful techniques into your daily routine can create a more harmonious and connected family life.

Finding Peace Amidst Chaos

Life can often feel like a whirlwind, with responsibilities tugging at you from every direction. Finding moments of peace and mindfulness during this chaos can seem nearly impossible, but it's achievable with the right techniques. Quick mindfulness breaks can be your lifeline. These are short pauses where you take a moment to center yourself. Close your eyes, take a few deep breaths, and focus on the sensation of the air filling your lungs. Even just 30 seconds of mindful breathing can make a significant difference. Another technique is to engage in a sensory check-in. Notice what you see, hear, smell, taste, and feel. This simple practice can ground you in the present moment and calm you.

Finding peace in everyday activities is another powerful way to integrate mindfulness into your life. Washing dishes, for example, can become a meditative practice. Pay attention to the water's warmth, the soap's feel, and the running tap's sound. This turns a mundane chore into a moment of mindfulness. A personal story that comes to mind is when I started practicing mindful walking on my way to work. Instead of rushing, I focused on the sensation of my feet hitting the pavement and the rhythm of my steps. This simple shift transformed my commute from a stressful rush to a peaceful start to my day.

Creating mindful spaces at home can also promote a sense of calm and tranquility. Setting up a home mindfulness corner doesn't require much space—just a small area where you can retreat for a few minutes of peace. Add a comfortable cushion, calming decorations, and perhaps a plant. The presence of natural elements like plants or water features can enhance the calming effect. Declutter techniques mindfully involve sorting items into categories: keep, donate, and discard. A clutter-free space can significantly reduce stress and create an environment conducive to mindfulness.

Practicing mindfulness on the go is essential for those of us with busy schedules. Mindful driving techniques can transform your commute into a peaceful experience. Focus on the sensation of your hands on the steering wheel, the rhythm of your breath, and the sights around you. Instead of getting frustrated with traffic, use that time to practice mindfulness. Walking meditation in busy environments is another way to stay centered. As you walk through a crowded street, focus on each step, the movement of your body, and the sounds around you. Using mindfulness apps on the go can provide guided practices and reminders to stay present, making it easier to incorporate mindfulness into your daily routine.

Cultivating a mindful attitude means integrating mindfulness into every aspect of your life, not just during formal practices. Practicing gratitude daily can shift your focus from what's wrong to what's right. Take a moment to reflect on three things you're grateful for each day. This simple practice can bring a sense of positivity and contentment. Techniques for mindful reflection at the end of the day involve reviewing your day with a non-judgmental attitude. Consider what went well, what challenges you faced, and how you handled them. Inspirational quotes and affirmations for daily mindfulness can serve as gentle reminders to stay present. Write down a few of your favorite quotes and place them where you'll see them often, such as on your bathroom mirror or computer screen.

Incorporating these practices into your life can help you find moments of peace and mindfulness, even amidst the chaos. By creating mindful spaces, practicing mindfulness on the go, and cultivating a mindful attitude, you can navigate the demands of daily life with greater ease and calm. This chapter has provided practical tools and techniques to balance your roles and responsibilities mindfully, reducing stress and enhancing your overall well-being.

EIGHT

Living in the Present Moment

I remember a summer afternoon when I sat in my backyard, watching my children play. My mind would have been racing about work deadlines, household chores, and future plans. But that day, something shifted. I decided to immerse myself fully in the moment. I noticed the vibrant colors of the flowers, the sound of laughter, and the sun's warmth on my skin. I felt a profound sense of peace and contentment for the first time in a long while. This experience taught me the transformative power of living in the present.

The Power of Now: Staying Present

Understanding Present-Moment Awareness: Living in the present moment, often referred to as present-moment awareness, means fully engaging with the here and now. It involves paying attention to your current experience rather than dwelling on the past or worrying about the future. This simple yet profound practice can significantly enhance your psychological and emotional well-being. Research shows that being present can lower stress levels, improve mood, and increase overall life satisfaction.

When you're present, you're not bogged down by regrets about the past or anxieties about the future. Instead, you experience life with all its beauty and imperfections as it unfolds. This can lead to greater emotional resilience, as you're better equipped to handle whatever comes your way without the added burden of past and future worries. Being present allows you to fully appreciate the small joys of life, which often go unnoticed when your mind is elsewhere.

Techniques for Staying Present: One of the most effective ways to stay anchored in the present is through mindful breathing exercises. These exercises help you connect with your breath, always in the here and now. Try this: Sit comfortably, close your eyes, and take a deep breath through your nose. Feel the air fill your lungs, and then slowly exhale through your mouth. Focus solely on the sensation of breathing, and let any wandering thoughts drift away.

Another powerful technique is using sensory awareness to stay grounded. Pay attention to the details around you—the texture of the fabric you're sitting on, the sounds in your environment, the taste of your food. Engaging your senses helps bring your mind back to the present moment. You can also redirect wandering thoughts by gently acknowledging them and then shifting your focus to what you are doing.

The Role of Acceptance: Acceptance plays a crucial role in staying present. It means embracing the present moment without trying to change or judge it. This non-judgmental awareness allows you to experience life more fully and respond to situations more clearly and calmly. Acceptance doesn't mean resignation; it means acknowledging reality without resistance.

Practicing acceptance can be challenging, especially when faced with difficult emotions or situations. But by accepting what is, you free yourself from the struggle against reality. Techniques for practicing acceptance include mindfulness meditation, where you observe your thoughts and feelings without getting caught up in them. You might say, "It's okay to feel this way. This moment is as it is." This simple acknowledgment can create a sense of peace and reduce the urge to control everything.

Real-Life Applications: Staying present can enhance various aspects of your life. At work, being present can improve focus and productivity. When fully engaged in a task, you're more likely to perform it efficiently and effectively. This focused attention can lead to better work quality and greater job satisfaction.

Being present fosters deeper connections in personal relationships. When you listen to someone with full attention without thinking about what to say next or getting distracted, you create a space for genuine understanding and empathy. This mindful communication can strengthen your relationships and make interactions more meaningful.

Finally, staying present helps you find joy in everyday activities. Whether it's savoring a meal, enjoying a walk, or playing with your children, being fully engaged in these moments can bring a sense of fulfillment and happiness. You begin to appreciate the richness of life's simple pleasures, often overlooked in daily life's rush.

Reflection Exercise: Savoring the Moment

Take a moment to reflect on a recent experience where you felt fully present. What were you doing? How did it feel? Write down your thoughts and consider how to bring more of these moments into your daily life.

Living in the present moment is a powerful practice that can transform your life. By embracing the here and now, you can reduce stress, improve your well-being, and find deeper connection and joy in your everyday experiences.

Letting Go of the Past

The past has a way of clinging to us, like an old coat we can't seem to shed. You might find yourself replaying past mistakes or regretting missed opportunities. This emotional weight can be heavy, making it hard to move forward. Past regrets and grudges can hinder your present happiness, keeping you in a negative cycle. Holding onto these feelings can also contribute to current stress, as unresolved issues from the past often manifest as anxiety or emotional turmoil in the present. Recognizing how these past experiences affect your well-being is the first step toward freeing yourself from their grip.

Mindfulness techniques can be incredibly effective in helping you release the hold of the past. Guided meditations for letting go can provide a structured way to process and release these lingering emotions. Close your eyes, take a deep breath, and visualize a moment you're struggling to let go of from your past. Picture it as a cloud drifting away, getting smaller and smaller until it disappears. This visualization can help you emotionally distance yourself from past events. Journaling exercises are another powerful tool. Write about your past experiences, allowing yourself to express your feelings fully. This act of writing can be cathartic, helping you process and make sense of your emotions. Visualizations for release and healing, such as imagining a healing light washing over you, can also facilitate emotional release and bring peace.

Forgiveness and self-compassion play crucial roles in letting go of the past. Practicing self-forgiveness allows you to acknowledge your mistakes without harsh self-judgment. One effective technique is to write a letter to yourself, offering the same kindness and understanding you would extend to a friend. This can help you move past self-blame and cultivate a sense of self-acceptance. Cultivating compassion for others is equally important. Holding onto grudges can be a heavy burden, but practicing compassion can lighten this load. Try to see the situation from the other person's perspective and understand their actions within the context of their struggles. Real-life stories of healing through forgiveness can be inspiring. Consider the story of a woman who forgave her estranged father after years of resentment. This act of forgiveness healed their relationship and brought her a profound sense of inner peace.

Moving forward involves setting intentions for the future and creating rituals for closure. Setting intentions can provide a sense of direction and purpose. Write down your intentions, focusing on the positive changes you want to make. Creating rituals for closure, such as lighting a candle or saying a prayer, can symbolize letting go of the past and embracing the present. Practicing gratitude for the present moment is another powerful strategy. Each day, take a moment to reflect on what you're grateful for. This can shift your focus from past regrets to present blessings, fostering a sense of contentment and peace.

Exercise: Writing a Letter of Forgiveness

Find a quiet space and take a few deep breaths to center yourself. Write a letter to someone from your past whom you need to forgive. You don't have to send it. Just the act of writing can help you process your feelings and find closure.

By recognizing the impact of the past, practicing mindfulness techniques, and embracing forgiveness and self-compassion, you can release the hold of past experiences and move forward with a lighter heart and a clearer mind.

Reducing Worry About the Future

Worrying about the future is something we all do, but it can be particularly intense for those of us who struggle with anxiety. Future anxiety stems from our brain's natural tendency to predict and plan. While this can be helpful, it often spirals into a cycle of worry when we fixate on potential problems or uncertainties. This kind of anxiety can be triggered by various factors—upcoming deadlines, financial concerns, health issues, or even the state of the world. When left unchecked, worrying about the future can significantly impact our mental health, leading to increased stress, insomnia, and even physical symptoms like headaches or digestive issues.

One of the most effective ways to manage future anxiety is through mindfulness practices. Simple guided breathing exercises can provide immediate relief. Find a quiet space, sit comfortably, and take a deep breath through your nose. Hold it for a moment, then slowly exhale through your mouth. Repeat this process several times, focusing solely on your breath. This can help calm your mind and body, reducing the intensity of your worries. Visualization techniques can also be incredibly soothing. Close your eyes and picture a peaceful scene—perhaps a serene beach or a quiet forest. Imagine yourself there, feeling safe and relaxed. This mental escape can help alleviate fears about the future.

Mindful journaling is another powerful tool for addressing future concerns. Set aside a few minutes each day to write about your worries. Be honest and specific about what's troubling you. Then, list possible solutions or steps you can take to address these concerns. This practice helps you process your emotions and brings clarity and perspective. You might find that some worries are not as daunting as they initially seemed, and others may have actionable steps you can take to mitigate them.

Cultivating trust in the process of life and practicing patience are essential for reducing future anxiety. It's about building trust in yourself and the universe. One technique for building this trust is to reflect on past challenges you've overcome. Remind yourself that you have navigated difficulties before and have the strength to do so again. Exercises for practicing patience can be woven into your daily life. For instance, when you find yourself in a situation that tests your patience—like waiting in line or dealing with a slow internet connection—take a deep breath and remind yourself that it's okay to wait. These small moments of patience can build your resilience over time.

Personal stories can be incredibly inspiring. I recall a friend who was facing a significant career transition. She was worried about whether she would find a new job that matched her skills and passions. By practicing mindfulness and cultivating trust, she learned to focus on the steps she could control, like updating her resume and networking. Over time, she found a job that she loved and realized that her worries, while valid, did not define her path. This experience underscored the importance of trusting the process and being patient with ourselves.

Shifting your focus from future worries to present-moment awareness can be a game-changer. One effective strategy is to redirect anxious thoughts when they arise. When you catch yourself worrying about the future, gently bring your attention back to the present moment. You might say to yourself, "Right now, I am safe. Right now, I am okay." Mindful activities can also help anchor you in the present. Engage in activities that require your full attention, like cooking, gardening, or drawing. These activities can provide a mental break from future worries and help you stay grounded.

Creating a daily mindfulness practice can further support your efforts to stay present. Start your day with a short meditation, focusing on your breath, or a calming mantra. Throughout the day, take mindful breaks to check in with yourself and reset your focus. Even a few minutes of mindfulness can make a significant difference. Integrating these practices into your routine allows you to gradually shift your mindset from future-focused anxiety to present-moment awareness, finding peace and balance in your daily life

Practicing Mindfulness in Everyday Activities

Incorporating mindfulness into your daily routine doesn't require grand gestures. It's about finding moments of presence in the mundane. When I first started practicing mindfulness, I discovered that everyday tasks could become opportunities for mindfulness. Cooking, for instance, became a meditative experience. As I chopped vegetables, I focused on the rhythm of the knife, the vibrant colors, and the fresh scents. Each step in the process grounded me in the present moment, transforming a routine chore into a source of calm and satisfaction.

Household chores can also become mindful activities. Whether you're washing dishes, folding laundry, or sweeping the floor, paying full attention to the task at hand can be surprisingly soothing. Feel the warm water on your hands, the fabric's texture, or the broom's movement. By immersing yourself in these sensations, you can quiet your mind and find a sense of peace in the simplicity of the task. Mindful commuting is another way to bring mindfulness into your daily life. Instead of stressing about traffic or getting lost in thought, focus on the sensations of driving or walking. Notice the sights, sounds, and smells around you. This shift in focus can turn your commute from a stressful experience into a mindful journey.

Mindful communication is essential for building deeper, more meaningful connections. Active listening exercises can transform how you interact with others. When someone is speaking to you, give them your full attention. Make eye contact, nod, and avoid interrupting. This shows respect and allows you to understand their perspective fully. Techniques for mindful speaking involve pausing before you respond, choosing your words carefully, and speaking with intention. Reflective listening practices can further enhance your interactions. Reflect on what you heard after someone shares their thoughts to ensure understanding. Phrases like "What I hear you saying is..." can clarify communication and deepen your connection.

Leisure activities offer another opportunity for mindfulness. Mindful reading, for example, involves immersing yourself fully in the text. Pay attention to the words, the emotions they evoke, and the imagery they create. This focused attention can make reading a more enriching experience. Similarly, practicing mindfulness during exercise can enhance your physical and mental well-being. Whether you're running, doing yoga, or lifting weights, focus on your breath, the movement of your body, and the sensations you feel. This not only improves your performance but also makes exercise more enjoyable. Mindful creative activities like painting or crafting can also be deeply fulfilling. Lose yourself in the process, noticing your creativity's colors, textures, and flow.

Creating mindful rituals can anchor your day in moments of presence and calm. A morning mindfulness routine can set a positive tone for the day. Start with a few minutes of meditation or deep breathing, then set an intention for the day. This practice can help you approach your day with clarity and purpose. Evening wind-down practices are equally important. Spend a few minutes reflecting on your day, acknowledging your accomplishments, and letting go of any lingering stress. Consider incorporating gentle stretches or soothing tea into your evening routine. Mindful moments throughout the day can sustain your practice. Take a few deep breaths before starting a new task, pause to appreciate a beautiful view, or savor the taste of your food. These small moments of mindfulness can accumulate, creating a more peaceful and centered life.

Exercise. Creating a Mindful Morning Routine

Start your day with intention. Spend five minutes each morning in silence, focusing on your breath. Set an intention for how you want to approach your day. Notice how this practice influences your mood and productivity.

Incorporating mindfulness into everyday activities can transform your routine, making each moment an opportunity for presence and peace. Practicing mindfulness in routine tasks, communication, leisure activities, and daily rituals can create a life filled with deeper connections, greater satisfaction, and lasting tranquility.

NINE

Guided Meditations for Specific Needs

I remember one particularly hectic day. Work was overwhelming, my kids demanded my attention, and my to-do list seemed endless. By late afternoon, I felt like I was about to implode. My shoulders were tense, my head was pounding, and I couldn't focus on anything. That's when I decided to try a guided meditation for stress relief. I found a quiet corner, closed my eyes, and followed the soothing voice guiding me through deep breathing and visualization. In just a few minutes, I felt a wave of calm wash over me, and the tension began to melt away. This experience showed me firsthand how powerful stress relief meditation can be.

Introduction to Stress Relief Meditation

Stress is a common part of life but often affects the body and mind. When stressed, your body goes into fight-or-flight mode, releasing stress hormones like cortisol. This response was useful for our ancestors when facing immediate dangers, but in modern life, it can lead to chronic stress and a host of related issues. Stress can manifest physically through headaches, muscle tension, and digestive problems. Emotionally, it can result in anxiety, irritability, and even depression.

Meditation offers a powerful antidote to stress. Meditation can counteract the stress response by focusing your mind and calming your body. It lowers cortisol levels, slows your heart rate, and helps relax your muscles. This practice can create a state of deep relaxation and mental clarity, allowing you to tackle life's challenges with a more balanced mindset.

Preparation for Meditation

Preparing your body and mind before you begin the meditation is important. First, find a quiet, comfortable space where you won't be disturbed. This could be a cozy corner of your home, a quiet room, or even a peaceful spot in your garden. The key is to choose a place where you feel safe and relaxed.

Setting a calming ambiance can enhance the meditation experience. Soft lighting, such as a dim lamp or candles, can create a soothing environment. Consider playing gentle, instrumental music or nature sounds to block background noise. Using props like cushions or blankets can also add to your comfort. Sit or lie comfortably, perhaps with a cushion supporting your back or a blanket draped over your legs.

Step-by-Step Meditation Guide

Now that you're ready, let's dive into the stress relief meditation. Start by closing your eyes and taking a few deep breaths. Inhale deeply through your nose, allowing your abdomen to expand, and then exhale slowly through your mouth. Repeat this a few times to center yourself and begin relaxing your body.

Next, we'll practice progressive muscle relaxation. Starting with your toes, tense the muscles for a few seconds and then release. Move up to your calves, thighs, and so on until you've tensed and relaxed each muscle group in your body. This technique helps release built-up tension and prepares your body for deeper relaxation.

Now, let's move into visualization. Imagine yourself in a peaceful place that brings you joy and tranquility. It could be a beach with gentle waves lapping at the shore, a lush forest with birds chirping, or a serene mountain top with a cool breeze. Picture every detail vividly —the colors, sounds, smells, and sensations. As you immerse yourself in this visualization, let any remaining tension melt away. Stay in this peaceful place for a few minutes, enjoying the sense of calm and relaxation.

Post-Meditation Practices

After the meditation, it's important to mindfully transition back to your day. Start with some gentle stretching exercises to awaken your body. Stretch your arms overhead, roll your shoulders, and gently twist your torso from side to side. These movements can help release any residual tension and re-energize you.

Consider drinking a cup of herbal tea to enhance your sense of calm further. Chamomile, lavender, or peppermint tea can be particularly soothing. As you sip your tea, take a moment to savor the warmth and flavor, practicing mindfulness by fully engaging with the experience.

Finally, take a few minutes to journal about your meditation experience. Reflect on how you felt before, during, and after the meditation. Note any physical or emotional changes you observed. Journaling can reinforce the benefits of meditation and provide a valuable record of your progress.

Guided meditation for stress relief can be a powerful tool for navigating life's challenges with greater ease and resilience. By incorporating these practices into your routine, you can create calm and clear moments, deepening your inner peace.

Guided Meditation for Self-Compassion

Self-compassion meditation is a powerful tool for fostering self-love and acceptance. It's not just about being kind to yourself superficially; it's about fundamentally changing how you relate to yourself, especially in moments of struggle. Self-compassion plays a crucial role in mental health by helping you respond to your suffering with kindness rather than harsh judgment. This practice can be transformative. It teaches you to treat yourself with the same care and understanding you would offer a close friend.

Imagine waking up each morning, and instead of criticizing yourself for not doing enough, you gently remind yourself that you're doing your best. Picture facing a difficult situation, and instead of berating yourself for feeling anxious, you place a hand over your heart and offer yourself words of encouragement. Self-compassion meditation fosters these moments of self-love, helping you to embrace your imperfections and see them as part of the shared human experience.

I've seen firsthand how self-compassion meditation can change lives. A friend who constantly struggled with feelings of inadequacy began practicing it. Over time, she started to notice a shift. She became more patient with herself, more forgiving of her mistakes, and more resilient in the face of challenges. Another woman I know, dealing with the aftermath of a painful divorce, found solace in self-compassion meditation. It helped her heal from the emotional wounds and rebuild her self-worth.

Creating a safe and nurturing environment is key to getting the most out of your self-compassion meditation practice. Start by choosing a quiet and private location where you won't be disturbed. This could be a cozy corner of your bedroom, a peaceful spot in your living room, or even a secluded area in your garden. Surround yourself with soft, comforting items like blankets, cushions, or a favorite stuffed animal. These items can provide a sense of security and comfort, helping you to relax more deeply.

Setting an intention for your meditation session can also be incredibly helpful. Before you begin, take a moment to reflect on what you hope to achieve. You may want to cultivate more self-love, find forgiveness for past mistakes, or offer yourself some kindness in a difficult moment. Setting an intention can give your meditation a sense of purpose and direction.

To begin the self-compassion meditation, start with mindful breathing to center your mind. Sit comfortably, close your eyes, and take a few deep breaths. Inhale deeply through your nose, feeling your abdomen expand, and then exhale slowly through your mouth. As you breathe, allow your mind to settle and your body to relax.

Next, start silently reciting self-compassion phrases. These could be phrases like, "May I be kind to myself," "May I accept myself as I am," or "May I find peace in my heart." Repeat these phrases slowly and gently, allowing their meaning to sink in. You might find it helpful to vary the phrases based on your needs.

As you breathe and recite phrases, visualize yourself surrounded by a warm, comforting light. This light represents the love and compassion you're offering to yourself. Imagine it enveloping you, filling you with warmth and peace. If it feels right, place your hands on your heart as a physical gesture of self-compassion. Feel the warmth of your hands and let it remind you that you deserve love and kindness.

Integrating self-compassion into your daily life can make a significant difference. During challenging moments, try using your self-compassion phrases. When you catch yourself in negative self-talk, pause and replace those critical thoughts with words of kindness. Practicing self-compassion in front of a mirror can also be powerful. Look into your own eyes and speak words of encouragement and love. This might initially feel awkward, but it can help reinforce a compassionate inner dialogue.

Keeping a self-compassion journal is another great way to integrate this practice into your life. Each day, write down moments when you offered yourself kindness or times when you struggled and how you responded. Reflect on these entries and notice any patterns or changes over time. This journal can serve as a reminder of your progress and a tool for deepening your self-compassion practice.

Guided Meditation for Emotional Balance

Emotional balance is crucial for overall well-being. It helps you navigate life's ups and downs with grace and resilience. You might feel overwhelmed, irritable, or anxious when your emotions are out of balance. These imbalances can affect your relationships, work, and physical health. Emotional balance meditation helps you maintain a steady emotional state, which in turn enhances your overall quality of life. Regularly practicing this type of meditation can achieve a more balanced emotional state, allowing you to respond to life's challenges calmly and clearly.

To prepare for an emotional balance meditation, creating a serene and clutter-free space is important. Choose a spot where you feel comfortable and safe. This could be a quiet corner of your home, a peaceful area in your garden, or even a dedicated meditation room. Clear away any clutter that might distract you. A tidy space can help create a sense of calm and order. Setting an intention for your meditation can also be helpful. Reflect on what you hope to achieve from the session. You may want to cultivate more patience, find inner peace, or become more aware of your emotions. Setting an intention can give your meditation a sense of purpose and direction. Using calming scents like lavender or chamomile can further enhance your meditation experience. These scents have calming properties that can help you relax and focus.

Let's move into the step-by-step guide for emotional balance meditation. Begin with grounding exercises. Sit comfortably and place your feet flat on the ground. Feel the connection between your feet and the earth. This grounding technique helps anchor you in the present moment. Next, take a few deep breaths. Inhale deeply through your nose, allowing your abdomen to expand, and then exhale slowly through your mouth. Repeat this a few times to center yourself. Now, mindfully observe your current emotions. Without judgment, acknowledge any feelings that arise. Whether it's sadness, joy, frustration, or contentment, let each emotion come and go without trying to change it. Use your breath to create a sense of balance and harmony. As you inhale, imagine drawing in calm and peace. As you exhale, visualize releasing any tension or negativity. Continue this rhythmic breathing, allowing your breath to steady your emotions.

Visualizing yourself in a state of emotional stability and calm can be incredibly powerful. Imagine yourself standing in a peaceful place, feeling balanced and centered. Picture a serene environment, whether it's a tranquil beach, a quiet forest, or a mountaintop. Envision yourself standing tall, with a sense of inner strength and calm. As you visualize this scene, let the feelings of stability and peace wash over you. Stay in this visualization for a few minutes, soaking in emotional balance and tranquility.

After completing the meditation, take some time for post-meditation reflection. Journaling about your current emotional state can deepen your understanding and awareness. Write down any emotions you observed during the meditation and how you felt before and after the session. Reflect on the impact of the meditation. Did you notice any shifts in your emotional state? Were there any particular emotions that stood out? Setting intentions for maintaining emotional balance can also be helpful. Think about how you can carry balance and calm into your daily life. Write down any intentions or affirmations that resonate with you. This practice can reinforce the benefits of meditation and support your ongoing emotional well-being.

By regularly practicing emotional balance meditation, you can develop a greater sense of emotional stability and resilience. This practice can help you navigate life's challenges with a calm and balanced mind, enhancing your overall well-being and inner peace.

Guided Meditation for Sleep

When I first tried sleep meditation, I was desperate for rest. Nights were filled with tossing and turning, my mind racing with worries and unfinished tasks. Like many women juggling multiple roles, I needed help to wind down. Sleep meditation became my sanctuary, a gentle way to transition from the day's chaos to a peaceful night's rest. The primary purpose of sleep meditation is to prepare your body and mind for restful sleep. It helps quiet the mental chatter, reduce stress, and create a relaxation conducive to deep, restorative sleep.

Poor sleep impacts every aspect of health. It can lead to irritability, difficulty concentrating, and weakened immune function. Chronic sleep deprivation is linked to more serious issues like heart disease, depression, and obesity. Meditation offers a natural way to improve sleep quality by calming the mind and relaxing the body. Through focused attention and deep breathing, meditation helps to lower the heart rate, reduce muscle tension, and signal to your body that it's time to sleep.

Creating a sleep-inducing environment is crucial for effective sleep meditation. Start by ensuring your sleeping space is dark, quiet, and cool. Darkness signals to your brain that it's time to produce melatonin, the hormone that regulates sleep. Blackout curtains or an eye mask can help block out light. Silence is equally important. Use earplugs or a white noise machine to drown out disruptive sounds. Soft, soothing music can also create a calming atmosphere. Incorporating scents like lavender or chamomile can further enhance relaxation. These scents are known for their calming properties and can help create a sense of tranquility.

To begin the sleep meditation, start with a body scan to release tension. Lie down comfortably on your bed and close your eyes. Take a few deep breaths, focusing on the sensation of air entering and leaving your lungs. Begin by directing your attention to your toes. Notice any tension or discomfort and consciously relax that area. Gradually move your focus through your body—your feet, legs, hips, abdomen, chest, arms, and head. As you scan each area, breathe deeply and release any tension.

Next, practice deep, slow breathing to calm your mind. Inhale deeply through your nose, filling your lungs completely. Hold your breath for a moment, then exhale slowly through your mouth. Repeat this process several times, making each breath slower and deeper. This breathing technique helps to lower your heart rate and create a sense of calm.

Now, visualize a peaceful, sleep-inducing scene. Imagine floating on a soft, fluffy cloud, gently swaying with the breeze. Feel the cloud supporting your body, cradling you in comfort. Picture the sky above, filled with twinkling stars, and feel the cool, fresh air on your skin. As you immerse yourself in this visualization, let any remaining tension melt away. Continue to breathe deeply, syncing your breath with the gentle movement of the cloud.

Using affirmations for restful sleep can further enhance the meditation. Silently repeat phrases like, "I am calm and ready for sleep," "My mind is at peace," or "I release the worries of the day."

These affirmations help to reinforce a sense of calm and readiness for sleep.

Maintaining a consistent sleep routine is essential for good sleep hygiene. Try to go to bed and wake up simultaneously every day, even on weekends. This helps regulate your body's internal clock. Avoid screens and stimulating activities before bed. The blue light from screens can interfere with melatonin production, making it harder to fall asleep. Instead, use calming activities like reading a book, taking a warm bath, or practicing gentle yoga or stretching. These activities can help signal your body that it's time to wind down.

Incorporating sleep meditation into your nightly routine can transform your sleep experience. By creating a sleep-inducing environment, practicing guided meditation techniques, and maintaining a consistent sleep schedule, you can improve the quality of your sleep and wake up feeling refreshed and rejuvenated.

Let's explore how integrating mindfulness into daily routines can create lasting peace and balance as we move forward.

TEN

Mindfulness During Life Transitions

Life is full of transitions, and one of the most challenging can be losing a job. I remember a time when I faced this difficult experience. Walking out of the office for the last time, I felt fear, anger, and sadness. The uncertainty of what lay ahead was overwhelming. I realized that to move forward, I needed to acknowledge and process these emotions mindfully. This chapter aims to guide you through this unsettling time with mindfulness techniques to help you manage the emotional upheaval and maintain your self-worth.

Coping with Job Loss

Losing a job can stir up a whirlwind of emotions. It's essential to mindfully acknowledge and process these feelings rather than suppress them. Start by identifying and labeling your emotions. Are you feeling angry, scared, or perhaps ashamed? Naming these feelings can help you understand and manage them better. This practice is known as emotional granularity, which involves being precise about your feelings. Instead of saying, "I'm upset," try to articulate, "I'm feeling frustrated and anxious about my financial stability." This clarity can reduce the intensity of your emotions by making them more manageable.

In moments of heightened emotional intensity, mindful breathing exercises can be incredibly grounding. Close your eyes and take a deep breath through your nose, feeling your lungs expand. Hold it for a moment, then exhale slowly through your mouth. Repeat this process a few times, focusing solely on the sensation of your breath. This simple act can help bring you back to the present moment, reducing the intensity of your emotions and offering a sense of calm amidst the chaos.

Journaling is another powerful tool for reflecting on your job loss experience. Set aside a few minutes daily to write about your thoughts and feelings. Don't worry about grammar or structure; just let your emotions flow onto the paper. You might write about the initial shock, the fears about the future, or even the small moments of hope you encounter. This practice can provide a safe space to process your emotions and gain insights into your experience. Over time, you may notice patterns or themes that can guide your healing process.

Maintaining your self-worth during job loss is crucial. It's easy to fall into the trap of equating your job with your value but remember, you are so much more than your employment status. Practice self-compassion by offering yourself the kindness and understanding you would give a friend in a similar situation. When feelings of failure arise, counteract them with self-compassion exercises. For instance, place your hand on your heart and gently remind yourself, "It's okay to feel this way. I am doing my best, and this situation does not define my worth."

Affirmations can also significantly reinforce self-worth. Create a set of affirmations that resonate with you, such as "I am capable and resilient" or "I have valuable skills and talents." Repeat these affirmations daily, especially during moments of doubt. This practice can help rewire your brain to focus on your strengths and potential rather than your perceived shortcomings.

Visualization techniques can further support your self-worth by helping you envision future success. Find a quiet place to sit comfortably, close your eyes, and take a few deep breaths. Imagine yourself thriving in a new job or career that excites and fulfills you. Picture the details—what you're doing, your environment, and the people you're working with. Allow yourself to feel the emotions associated with this success—joy, pride, and satisfaction. Visualization can create a mental blueprint for your goals, making them feel more attainable.

Staying present and focused can be particularly challenging during job loss, as worries about the future often dominate your thoughts. Incorporate mindful job search practices to keep you grounded. Set specific times for job hunting and related activities; use that time mindfully. Focus on one task at a time, whether updating your resume, writing a cover letter, or searching for job openings. This focused approach can prevent you from feeling overwhelmed and increase your productivity.

Managing anxiety about future employment is another critical aspect. Techniques such as mindful breathing and grounding exercises can help. For example, before an interview, take a few moments to practice deep breathing or the 5-4-3-2-1 grounding technique: identify five things you can see, four you can touch, three you can hear, two you can smell, and one you can taste. These practices can help calm your nerves and keep you focused on the present moment.

Establishing a new daily routine incorporating mindfulness can provide structure and stability during this uncertain time. Start by setting a regular schedule for job search activities. Dedicate specific hours of the day to searching for jobs, networking, or enhancing your skills. Include mindfulness breaks throughout the day to prevent burnout and maintain emotional well-being. During these breaks, practice a quick meditation, take a mindful walk, or take a few deep breaths.

Mindful morning and evening routines can further support your well-being. In the morning, start your day with a few minutes of meditation or deep breathing to set a positive tone. Reflect on your intentions for the day and visualize positive outcomes. In the evening, wind down with a gratitude practice. Reflect on three things you are grateful for, no matter how small. This practice can shift your focus from what you lack to what you have, fostering a sense of contentment and peace.

Losing a job is undeniably challenging, but with these mindfulness practices, you can navigate this transition with greater ease and resilience. By acknowledging and processing your emotions, maintaining your self-worth, staying present and focused, and creating a new routine, you can find a sense of stability and inner peace amidst the uncertainty.

Navigating Relationship Changes

Navigating relationship changes can be one of life's most challenging experiences. Whether it's the end of a romantic relationship, shifts in friendships, or evolving family dynamics, these changes can stir up a whirlwind of emotions. Mindful communication is one of the most effective ways to manage these transitions. When emotions run high, it's easy to miscommunicate or avoid communication altogether. Practicing active listening can make a world of difference. This means fully focusing on the other person when they speak, resisting the urge to interrupt, and reflecting on what you've heard. For instance, instead of immediately responding with your own perspective, you might say, "I hear that you're feeling hurt because I didn't call you back. I understand how that could be frustrating."

Expressing your own emotions mindfully is equally important. Techniques such as using "I" statements can reduce conflict and foster understanding. For example, instead of saying, "You never listen to me," try, "I feel unheard when I'm interrupted." This approach focuses on your feelings rather than placing blame, making it easier for the other person to hear and understand your perspective. It helps create a space for open and honest communication, crucial for resolving conflicts and building stronger relationships.

Managing emotional overload during relationship changes is another critical aspect. Guided meditations can be incredibly helpful for calming intense emotions. Find a quiet space, close your eyes, and focus on your breath. Imagine a gentle wave washing over you, carrying away your stress and leaving you feeling calm and centered. This practice can help you regain control over your emotions, making it easier to navigate difficult conversations.

Grounding techniques can also be beneficial during emotionally charged conversations. When you feel overwhelmed, try grounding yourself by focusing on the physical sensations in your body. Place your feet firmly on the ground, feel the support of the chair beneath you, or hold a comforting object. These simple actions can help you stay present and calm, allowing you to respond thoughtfully rather than impulsively. Additionally, practicing self-compassion during these times is crucial. Offer yourself the same kindness and understanding you would give a friend in a similar situation. Remind yourself that it's okay to feel a range of emotions and that you're doing your best.

Finding inner peace amidst relationship turmoil can seem daunting, but mindfulness provides a path forward. Mindful breathing exercises are a simple yet powerful tool for finding calm. Take a few moments each day to focus on your breath. Inhale deeply through your nose, hold for a moment, and exhale slowly through your mouth. This practice can help you release tension and find a sense of tranquility, even in chaos.

Visualization techniques can also create a mental sanctuary where you can retreat when emotions become overwhelming. Close your eyes and imagine a place where you feel safe and at peace. It could be a quiet beach, a lush forest, or a cozy room. Picture every detail—the colors, sounds, scents—and allow yourself to immerse in this peaceful space. This mental escape can provide a much-needed break from the stress of relationship changes.

Daily gratitude practices can shift your focus from the turmoil to the positive aspects of your life. Each evening, reflect on three things you are grateful for, no matter how small. It could be a kind word from a friend, a beautiful sunset, or a moment of laughter. This practice helps reframe your mindset, fostering appreciation and contentment even during challenging times.

Rebuilding and moving forward after a relationship change requires intention and mindfulness. Start by setting intentions for personal growth. Reflect on what you want to achieve and how you want to grow from this experience. Write down your intentions and revisit them regularly to stay focused on your goals. Mindful journaling can be a powerful tool for processing and healing. Set aside time each day to write about your thoughts and feelings. Don't worry about structure or grammar; just let your emotions flow onto the paper. This practice can help you gain clarity and insight, making it easier to move forward.

Another important step is creating a vision for the future. Take some time to imagine what you want your life to look like. Think about your goals, dreams, and aspirations. Visualize yourself achieving these goals and living the life you desire. This practice can help you stay motivated and focused on the possibilities ahead.

Embracing Health Challenges

Health challenges can be daunting, but practicing mindful acceptance can help you navigate this difficult terrain. Accepting the present moment without judgment involves acknowledging your current state without wishing it were different. For instance, if you're dealing with chronic pain, instead of focusing on how unfair it feels, try to observe the sensations objectively. Techniques like the body scan meditation can be particularly helpful. Lie down in a comfortable position, close your eyes, and slowly bring your attention to each part of your body, starting from your toes and moving up to your head. As you focus on each area, notice the sensations without labeling them as "good" or "bad." This practice can help you develop a more neutral and accepting attitude toward your physical condition.

Guided meditations focused on acceptance can also be beneficial. Find a quiet space, sit comfortably, and close your eyes. Begin by taking a few deep breaths to center yourself. Then, imagine a soft, warm light enveloping your body, bringing a sense of peace and acceptance. As you breathe in, say to yourself, "I accept this moment as it is." As you breathe out, let go of any tension or resistance. This meditation can help you cultivate a sense of calm and acceptance, even amidst physical discomfort.

I've met individuals who have embraced their health challenges with remarkable grace. One woman I know, diagnosed with a chronic illness, used mindfulness to transform her relationship with her body. Instead of battling against her condition, she learned to work with it, focusing on what she could do rather than what she couldn't. Her story is a testament to the power of mindful acceptance in finding peace and resilience.

Managing physical pain through mindfulness requires specific techniques. As mentioned earlier, the body scan meditation can serve as a valuable tool for pain relief. By focusing on different parts of your body, you can become more aware of your pain and how it shifts and changes. This awareness can help reduce the intensity of the pain, making it more manageable.

Another effective strategy is to redirect your focus away from pain. Instead of focusing on the pain, concentrate on other sensations or activities. For example, engage in a hobby or immerse yourself in a good book. This diversion can help shift your attention away from the pain, providing temporary relief.

Mindful breathing exercises can also reduce pain perception. Sit comfortably, close your eyes, and take a deep breath in through your nose. Hold it for a moment, then exhale slowly through your mouth. As you breathe, focus on the sensation of the air entering and leaving your body. Visualize the breath as a wave of soothing energy, washing over your pain and bringing relief. Repeat this process for a few minutes, and notice how your pain levels change.

Building emotional resilience during health challenges is crucial for maintaining your mental well-being. Loving-kindness meditation can be a powerful practice for fostering resilience. Sit comfortably, close your eyes, and take a few deep breaths. Begin by silently repeating loving-kind phrases to yourself, such as "May I be healthy. May I be strong. May I be at peace." After a few minutes, extend these wishes to others, starting with loved ones and gradually including neutral people and even difficult individuals. This practice can help cultivate compassion and connection, boosting emotional resilience.

Daily affirmations can also strengthen your resilience. Create a set of affirmations that resonate with your situation, such as "I am strong and capable" or "I have the inner resources to face this challenge." Repeat these affirmations daily, especially during moments of doubt or fear. This practice can help reinforce positive beliefs about yourself and your coping ability.

Journaling prompts provide a structured way to reflect on your personal growth. Set aside time each day to write about your experiences, focusing on how you've grown and what you've learned. Prompts like "What challenges have I overcome today?" or "What strengths have I discovered in myself?" can guide your reflections and help you recognize your resilience.

Integrating mindfulness into your medical treatment and self-care routines can enhance your well-being. During medical procedures, practice mindful breathing to stay calm and centered. Focus on your breath, and let it be an anchor, grounding you in the present moment. This can help reduce anxiety and make the experience more manageable.

Staying present during doctor's appointments can also be beneficial. Before your appointment, take a few deep breaths to calm your mind. Focus on the conversation during the appointment, actively listen to your doctor, and ask questions. This mindful approach can help you stay engaged and make informed decisions about your treatment.

Creating a mindfulness-based self-care plan can further support your health journey. Include meditation, mindful breathing, and gentle yoga in your daily routine. Set aside specific times for these activities, making them a regular part of your self-care regimen. This plan can provide structure and stability, helping you navigate your health challenges with greater ease and resilience.

Finding Stability in Uncertain Times

Life can sometimes feel like an unpredictable storm, tossing you around with waves of uncertainty. Finding stability during these times can make a world of difference. Sensory grounding techniques are one of the most effective ways to ground yourself. The 5-4-3-2-1 method is a practical tool to help you refocus on the present moment. Start by identifying five things you can see around you. Next, touch four different objects and notice their textures. Listen for three distinct sounds, smell two different scents, and focus on one thing you can taste. This method engages all your senses, returning you to the here and now.

Physical grounding exercises can also provide stability. Walking barefoot on grass or sand allows you to connect with the earth and feel its stability beneath you. Another technique is to press your feet firmly into the ground while sitting or standing, feeling the support beneath you. Visualization exercises can create a mental safe haven. Close your eyes and imagine a place where you feel secure and calm. This could be a cozy room, a serene beach, or a peaceful forest. Picture every detail, from the colors to the sounds, and immerse yourself fully in this stable, safe place.

Decision-making during uncertain times can be challenging. Mindfulness can offer clarity and calmness. Before making any decision, practice mindful breathing. Take a few deep breaths, inhaling through your nose and exhaling through your mouth. This simple act can help clear your mind and reduce anxiety. Observing your thoughts without judgment is another valuable technique. When faced with a decision, take a moment to notice the thoughts that arise. Are they based on fear or rational assessment? By observing without judgment, you can gain a clearer perspective.

Guided meditations can further enhance your decision-making process. Find a quiet space, sit comfortably, and close your eyes. Focus on your breath, and as you breathe in and out, allow your mind to settle. Visualize a calm, clear lake. Imagine dropping a question or decision into the lake and watching the ripples settle. As the water becomes still again, notice any insights or clarity that arise.

This practice can help you approach decisions with a calm and focused mind.

Creating a stable daily routine is crucial for maintaining balance during uncertain times. Start by setting a regular schedule that includes mindful activities. Dedicate specific times for meditation, exercise, and relaxation. These activities provide structure and predictability, helping you easily navigate your day. Including mindfulness breaks throughout the day can prevent stress from building up. Take a few minutes to step away from your tasks, close your eyes, and focus on your breath or a calming visualization. This can help you recharge and maintain your focus.

Mindful morning and evening routines can further enhance your stability. Begin your day with a few minutes of meditation or deep breathing to set a positive tone. Reflect on your intentions for the day and visualize positive outcomes. In the evening, wind down with a gratitude practice. Reflect on three things you are grateful for, no matter how small. This practice can shift your focus from what you lack to what you have, fostering a sense of contentment and peace.

Building a support network is another essential aspect of finding stability. Mindful communication techniques can help you build and strengthen relationships. Practice active listening by fully focusing on the other person when they speak, resisting the urge to interrupt, and reflecting on what you've heard. This fosters genuine understanding and connection. Techniques for practicing empathy and active listening can further enhance your relationships. Show empathy by acknowledging the other person's feelings and offering support.

Creating a community of mindfulness practitioners can provide additional support. Join or form a mindfulness group where you can share experiences, practice together, and offer mutual support. This sense of community can provide a stable foundation during uncertain times, helping you feel connected and supported.

Finding stability in uncertain times is about grounding yourself, making clear decisions, creating a stable routine, and building a supportive network. These mindfulness practices can help you navigate life's unpredictability with greater ease and resilience. As you continue to explore these techniques, you'll find that stability and inner peace are within your reach, even amidst the chaos.

ELEVEN

Integrating Mindfulness into Daily Routines

One morning, I was rushing through my routine, unaware of what I was doing. I spilled coffee on my favorite shirt, snapped at my kids, and left the house feeling frazzled and irritable. This chaotic start set the tone for the rest of my day, leaving me anxious and overwhelmed. I realized I needed a change. That's when I decided to incorporate mindfulness into my mornings. This simple shift transformed my entire day, bringing a sense of calm and balance I desperately needed.

Morning Mindfulness Rituals

Starting your day with intention can set a positive tone, helping you navigate the challenges ahead with grace and resilience. When you wake up, rather than immediately diving into your to-do list, take a moment to set a mindful intention. This practice involves pausing to reflect on what you hope to achieve emotionally and mentally throughout the day. For instance, you may focus on staying calm during stressful moments or being fully present with your family. Setting intentions can be done through a short meditation or simply sitting quietly and thinking about your goals. Affirmations can also be powerful. Start your day with positive statements like, "I am capable," or "I approach today calmly and confidently." Reflecting on your goals during morning meditation helps solidify these intentions, creating a mental roadmap for your day.

Incorporating specific mindfulness practices into your morning routine can further enhance this sense of calm. Begin with morning breathing exercises. As soon as you wake up, sit in bed or find a comfortable spot, close your eyes, and take several deep breaths. Focus on the sensation of the air filling your lungs and the rise and fall of your chest. This simple act can ground you and set a peaceful tone for the day. Stretching or yoga with mindful awareness is another excellent practice. Spend a few minutes stretching your body, paying attention to how each movement feels. Yoga poses like the cat-cow stretch or child's pose can be particularly soothing. If you prefer a more structured routine, follow a short yoga video that emphasizes mindfulness. Even a mindful shower can become a moment of tranquility. As you wash, focus on the sensation of the water on your skin, the smell of the soap, and the sound of the water. This practice turns a mundane task into a meditative experience.

Breakfast is another opportunity to practice mindfulness and set a calm tone for the day. Instead of rushing through your meal, take time to savor each bite. Notice the flavors, textures, and smells of your food. Pay attention to the eating experience rather than letting your mind wander to your day's tasks. This can be as simple as slowly eating a piece of fruit, noticing its sweetness, and appreciating its freshness. Practicing gratitude for your meal can also enhance this experience. Before you eat, take a moment to reflect on your food journey from farm to table and express gratitude for the nourishment it provides. This small act of mindfulness can transform your breakfast into a peaceful ritual, setting a positive tone for the rest of your day.

Creating a dedicated space for morning mindfulness rituals can make these practices more effective and enjoyable. Find a quiet corner in your home where you can retreat each morning. Set up this space with cushions and candles to create a cozy and inviting atmosphere. Incorporating calming elements like plants or crystals can enhance the tranquility of your mindfulness corner. Plants bring a touch of nature indoors, providing a sense of peace and grounding. Whether you believe in their healing properties or simply appreciate their beauty, Crystals can add a soothing energy to your space. Creating a morning meditation nook doesn't require much space—just a small area to sit comfortably and focus on your breath. Having a dedicated space for mindfulness can make it easier to establish and maintain your morning rituals.

To help you incorporate these practices into your routine, here's a simple checklist for a mindful morning:

Morning Mindfulness Checklist

- Take a few deep breaths as soon as you wake up.
- Set a mindful intention for the day.
- Use positive affirmations to boost your mood.
- Spend a few minutes stretching or practicing yoga.
- Take a mindful shower, focusing on the sensations.
- Savor your breakfast, paying attention to flavors and textures.
- Express gratitude for your meal.
- Spend a few minutes in your dedicated mindfulness space.

Starting your day with these mindful practices can transform your mornings from chaotic to calm. By setting intentions, practicing mindfulness, and creating a dedicated space, you can approach each day with peace and purpose.

Mindfulness During Work Hours

The daily commute can often feel like a necessary evil, but it doesn't have to be. Whether driving, walking, or using public transportation, this time can become an opportunity for mindfulness. If you're driving, mindful driving practices can transform your experience. Focus on the feel of the steering wheel, the rhythm of your breath, and the sights around you. Pay attention to the movement of your body as you steer and accelerate, noticing how your muscles engage and relax. Listening to calming music or a mindfulness podcast can also help you stay present and relaxed during your drive.

For those who walk to work, walking meditation offers a fantastic way to start the day mindfully. As you walk, focus on each step, the movement of your body, and the sensations under your feet. Notice the rhythm of your breath and how it syncs with your steps. Pay attention to your surroundings—the chirping of birds, the rustling of leaves, the feel of the breeze. If you use public transportation, this time can also be a moment for mindfulness meditation. Find a comfortable seat, close your eyes, and focus on your breath. Notice the sounds around you without judgment, letting them come and go like waves. You can also practice body scanning to release tension from your toes and move up to your head.

Once you arrive at work, taking mindful breaks throughout the day is crucial. These breaks help you reset and maintain focus. One effective technique is mindful breathing during breaks. Close your eyes, take a deep breath through your nose, and exhale slowly through your mouth. Repeat this a few times, focusing on the sensation of your breath. This simple practice can calm your mind and reduce stress. Stretching exercises at your desk can also be beneficial. Stand up, stretch your arms overhead, roll your shoulders, and twist your torso gently. These movements release physical tension and refresh your body.

Brief meditation sessions for re-centering can be incredibly effective. Find a quiet spot, even if it's just a bathroom stall or a corner of the office. Close your eyes, take a few deep breaths, and focus on the present moment. You might visualize a peaceful scene, like a beach or a forest, to help create a mental sanctuary. These short sessions help you regain focus and approach your work calmly.

Incorporating mindfulness into your work tasks can also make a significant difference. Practicing single-tasking instead of multitasking is a great place to start. Focus on one task at a time, giving it your full attention. This approach not only increases productivity but also reduces stress. Use mindful listening during meetings. Pay attention to the speaker, make eye contact, and nod to show understanding. Avoid interrupting, and take a moment to process what you've heard before responding. This practice fosters better communication and reduces misunderstandings. Techniques for maintaining focus and reducing distractions include setting specific times for checking emails, turning off non-essential notifications, and creating a dedicated workspace free from distractions.

Managing work stress with mindfulness practices can help you maintain calm during work hours. Mindful breathing techniques, such as the 4-7-8 breathing method, can be particularly effective for stress relief. Inhale for a count of four, hold for seven and exhale for eight. This practice activates the parasympathetic nervous system, promoting relaxation. Visualization exercises for creating a mental sanctuary can also be helpful. Close your eyes and imagine a place where you feel completely at peace. It could be a beach, a forest, or a cozy room. Spend a few minutes visualizing this place, noticing the colors, sounds, and sensations. This mental escape can provide a break from stress.

Journaling about work-related stress and solutions is another powerful tool. Take a few minutes each day to write about the challenges you faced and how you responded to them. Reflect on what worked well and didn't, and consider how you might handle similar situations. This practice helps you process your experiences and fosters a proactive approach to stress management.

Integrating these mindfulness practices into your workday can transform your experience, reducing stress and enhancing your overall well-being. You can create a more balanced and fulfilling work life by approaching your commute, breaks, tasks, and stress with mindfulness.

Evening Wind-Down Practices

The transition from work to home can often feel abrupt and jarring, leaving you carrying the stress of the day into your evening. One effective way to mentally close the workday is to establish a clear boundary between work and home life. Begin by setting a specific time to stop work-related activities. At this moment, take a few minutes to sit quietly and reflect on the day. Acknowledge your accomplishments and let go of unfinished tasks, knowing they can be addressed tomorrow. This practice can help you mentally close the workday, reducing the tendency to ruminate on work issues during your time.

Practice mindful commuting as you commute home, whether by car, public transport, or walking. If you're driving, focus on the feel of the steering wheel, the rhythm of your breath, and the sights around you. Try to let go of the day's stress with each exhale. For public transport, find a seat, close your eyes if you can, and focus on your breath or the sounds around you. Walking home offers a great opportunity for walking meditation. Pay attention to each step, the movement of your body, and the sensations under your feet. These mindful commuting practices can help you transition smoothly from work to home life.

Creating a ritual to signify the end of the workday can further reinforce this transition. It could be as simple as changing your clothes, washing your face, or lighting a candle. These small acts signal to your mind and body that the workday is over and it's time to relax. For example, a friend changes into her most comfortable clothes and makes a cup of herbal tea when she gets home. This simple ritual helps her leave work behind and shift into relaxation mode.

Mindful evening activities are essential for unwinding and preparing for a restful night. Cooking dinner can become a mindful practice. Focus on chopping vegetables, the smell of spices, and the sizzle of food in the pan. When you sit down to eat, savor each bite, paying attention to the flavors, textures, and smells. This practice enhances your dining experience and helps you stay present and enjoy the moment. Engaging in a hobby with mindful awareness can also be incredibly relaxing. Whether knitting, painting, or playing a musical instrument, focus fully on the activity. Notice the feel of the yarn, the paint's colors, or the music's sound. This mindful engagement can provide a sense of calm and fulfillment.

Gentle evening yoga or stretching routines are another excellent way to unwind. Spend a few minutes stretching your body, focusing on how each movement feels. Poses like a child's pose, legs up the wall, and gentle twists can help release tension and prepare your body for sleep. Practicing these movements with mindful awareness enhances their relaxing effects, helping you release the day's stress.

Preparing for a restful night's sleep involves incorporating mindfulness practices that promote deep relaxation. Evening meditation or a body scan can be particularly effective. Find a comfortable position, close your eyes, and focus on your breath. Gradually scan your body from head to toe, noticing any areas of tension and consciously relaxing them. Guided visualization exercises for sleep can also be helpful. Imagine a peaceful scene, like a beach or forest, and immerse yourself in the details. This mental escape can help quiet your mind and prepare you for sleep. Techniques for releasing the day's stress before bed include writing down any lingering thoughts or worries in a journal. This practice can help clear your mind, making it easier to drift off to sleep.

Creating a calming sleep environment is crucial for promoting mindfulness and relaxation. Start by setting up a calming bedroom ambiance with soft lighting and soothing scents. Use dim lamps or candles to create a gentle, relaxing atmosphere. Essential oils like lavender or chamomile can be diffused to promote relaxation. Using weighted blankets or other comfort items can also enhance your sleep environment. Weighted blankets provide a sense of security and can help reduce anxiety. Removing electronics and creating a screen-free zone is another important step. The blue light from screens can interfere with your body's natural sleep-wake cycle. Instead, enjoy calming activities like reading a book, listening to soothing music, or practicing gentle stretches before bed. Screen-free time helps signal your body that it's time to wind down and prepare for sleep.

Weekly Mindfulness Check-In

Reflecting on the week is a powerful way to stay grounded and mindful. Each weekend, sit quietly with your journal and reflect on the past seven days. Start by considering what went well. Did you manage to stay present during a particularly stressful meeting? You may find a few moments of peace during your morning commute. Write these successes down. They are worth celebrating. Next, think about the areas where you struggled. Perhaps you needed help maintaining focus during the afternoon slump or felt overwhelmed by your to-do list. Acknowledge these challenges without judgment. Use journaling prompts to guide your reflection, such as "What moments this week brought me joy?" or "When did I feel most stressed?" This practice helps you gain insight into your mindfulness journey, showing you where you're thriving and where you might need a little more attention.

Setting mindful intentions for the upcoming week can give you a clear and purposeful direction. Start by thinking about what you want to achieve mentally and emotionally. Your intentions should be realistic and meaningful, focusing on how you want to feel rather than specific outcomes. For example, instead of completing a project by mid-week, aim to approach your work calmly and focus. Techniques for creating these intentions include visualizing a successful week ahead. Picture yourself navigating your days with ease and grace, handling challenges calmly. Reinforce these intentions with affirmations. Write statements like, "I am capable of managing my time effectively," or "I will approach each task with mindfulness and patience." These affirmations help solidify your intentions, making them a guiding force throughout the week.

Incorporating mindfulness into your weekly planning and scheduling can help you create a balanced and fulfilling routine. Start by reviewing your commitments and identifying where you can integrate mindfulness practices. Techniques for mindful time management include setting aside specific times for mindfulness breaks, such as a short meditation before lunch or a mindful walk in the afternoon. Create a balanced schedule that includes both work and self-care activities. For instance, if you have a busy Tuesday day, plan a relaxing evening activity like a warm bath or gentle yoga session to unwind. Planning mindful activities and self-care can help you maintain balance and prevent burnout. Make sure to include activities that bring you joy and relaxation, whether reading a book, gardening, or spending time with loved ones.

Self-care and rejuvenation are crucial aspects of the weekly check-in. Reflect on your self-care needs and consider how to meet them in the upcoming week. This might involve setting boundaries to protect your time and energy or scheduling activities that nourish your mind and body. Techniques for identifying self-care needs include listening to your body and noticing how you feel. Are you tired and need rest, or do you crave social connection? Plan self-care activities that align with these needs. Consider activities like a spa day at home, a nature walk, or a creative hobby for relaxation and rejuvenation. Practicing gratitude for the week's experiences can also enhance your well-being. Take a moment to reflect on the positive aspects of your week and express gratitude for them. This practice can shift your focus from what went wrong to what went right, fostering a more positive outlook.

Here's a reflection exercise to help you with your weekly mindfulness check-in:

Weekly Reflection Exercise

1. Celebrate Successes: Write down three moments from the past week where you felt mindful and present.
2. Identify Challenges: Note any situations where you struggled to maintain mindfulness. What contributed to these challenges?
3. Set Intentions: Write down one or two mindful intentions for the upcoming week. How do you want to feel? What mindset do you want to cultivate?
4. Plan Self-Care: List three self-care activities you will prioritize in the coming week. How will these activities support your well-being?

Ending each week with this mindful check-in can provide valuable insights, helping you grow and improve your mindfulness practice. You can create a more balanced and fulfilling life by reflecting on your experiences, setting meaningful intentions, planning mindfully, and prioritizing self-care. This practice enhances your mindfulness journey and supports your overall well-being, helping you navigate life's challenges with greater ease and grace.

TWELVE

Holistic Well-Being and Inclusivity

I remember a time when everything felt disconnected. My mind was always racing, my emotions were everywhere, and my body often felt like it was carrying the world's weight. It wasn't until I started exploring the mind-body connection that I understood how intertwined our mental, emotional, and physical health are. This realization was a game-changer. It showed me a path to a more balanced and fulfilling life.

Understanding the Mind-Body Connection

The concept of the mind-body connection is not new, but it often feels like a profound revelation when you experience it personally. The mind-body connection refers to the relationship between our thoughts, emotions, and physical health. Our mental state can significantly influence our physical state and vice versa. Historically, figures like Galen and Moses Maimonides recognized this link, and modern science has only bolstered these ancient insights.

Scientific research supports the idea that our thoughts and emotions can have a direct impact on our physical health. Studies have shown that stress, for instance, affects the autonomic nervous system and neuroendocrine function, leading to various health issues, including heart disease and diabetes (SOURCE 1). When we experience psychological stress, our body releases stress hormones like cortisol, which can cause inflammation and weaken the immune system. Over time, chronic stress can lead to damaging changes in organ systems, contributing to conditions such as hypertension, digestive problems, and even depression.

Understanding how deeply our thoughts and emotions impact our physical well-being is crucial. When you're anxious or stressed, your body responds by tightening muscles, increasing heart rate, and triggering a cascade of stress hormones. Conversely, when you practice mindfulness and positive thinking, your body can relax, reduce stress hormone levels, and promote healing. This intricate dance between mind and body underscores the importance of holistic well-being.

Benefits of a Strong Mind-Body Connection

Cultivating a strong mind-body connection offers numerous benefits. First and foremost, it can significantly improve your mental health and emotional regulation. When you're attuned to your body's signals, you can better manage anxiety, stress, and emotional fluctuations. This heightened awareness helps you respond to challenges with a calm and balanced mindset rather than reacting impulsively.

Another notable benefit is enhanced physical health. A strong mind-body connection can reduce chronic pain and improve overall physical well-being. For instance, mindful practices like meditation and yoga have been shown to lower blood pressure, improve heart health, and boost immune function. By paying attention to your body's needs and responding with care and compassion, you can alleviate physical discomfort and promote healing.

Overall well-being and life satisfaction also improve when you nurture this connection. When you feel physically healthy and emotionally balanced, you're more likely to experience a sense of fulfillment and joy in your daily life. This holistic approach to well-being fosters a deeper appreciation for the present moment and a greater sense of inner peace.

Mindfulness Techniques to Strengthen the Connection

Several mindfulness techniques can help you strengthen the mind-body connection. One effective practice is body scan meditation, which involves paying close attention to different parts of your body, from your toes to the top of your head. This practice helps you become aware of physical sensations, areas of tension, and overall body awareness. By regularly tuning into your body, you can better understand its needs and respond with care.

Mindful breathing is another powerful technique. By focusing on your breath, you can synchronize your mind and body, creating a sense of harmony and balance. Deep, intentional breathing helps calm the nervous system, reduce stress, and improve mental clarity. Practicing mindful breathing throughout the day, especially during stressful moments, can help you stay grounded and centered.

Visualization exercises also enhance the mind-body connection. These exercises involve imagining peaceful and healing scenes, such as a serene beach or a lush forest. By visualizing these calming environments, you can evoke a sense of relaxation and well-being in your body. Visualization can also mentally rehearse positive outcomes, boosting confidence and reducing anxiety.

Real-Life Applications

The benefits of a strong mind-body connection extend to various aspects of life. For instance, athletes often use mindful movement techniques to improve their performance. Focusing on their breath and bodily sensations can enhance their coordination, stamina, and overall physical capabilities. This mindful approach helps them stay present and perform at their best.

Other significant benefits include enhanced creativity and problem-solving ability. When your mind and body are in sync, you can tap into a deeper well of creativity and innovation. Mindfulness practices help clear mental clutter, allowing you to think more clearly and approach problems with fresh perspectives. This heightened creativity can benefit both personal and professional endeavors.

Better stress management and resilience are the most impactful benefits of a strong mind-body connection. In the face of life's challenges, being attuned to your body and emotions helps you navigate stress with grace and poise. Mindfulness practices equip you with the tools to remain calm, centered, and resilient, even in the most trying times. This resilience improves your well-being and enhances your ability to support and connect with others.

Reflection Exercise: Exploring Your Mind-Body Connection

Take a few moments to reflect on your current mind-body connection. Sit in a quiet space, close your eyes, and take a few deep breaths. Pay attention to any sensations in your body—tension, warmth, coolness. Notice how your thoughts and emotions might be influencing these sensations. Write down your observations and consider incorporating mindfulness practices to strengthen this connection. This exercise can help you develop a deeper awareness of your mind-body relationship and guide you toward holistic well-being.

Mindful Stretching Exercises

Mindful stretching is more than just a series of physical movements. It's an intentional practice that blends the benefits of stretching with mindfulness to create a holistic mind and body experience. This practice involves paying close attention to the sensations in your body as you stretch, noticing how each movement feels, and staying present in the moment. Unlike traditional stretching, which often focuses solely on physical flexibility or exercise preparation, mindful stretching cultivates mental relaxation and emotional balance. It's about connecting with your body, easing tension, and finding calm.

The benefits of mindful stretching are numerous. Physically, it enhances flexibility and reduces muscle tension, alleviating pain and improving overall mobility. Mentally, it promotes relaxation, reduces stress, and enhances your awareness of how your body feels. Integrating mindfulness into your stretching routine can also improve your emotional well-being, as this practice encourages you to be kind and patient with yourself. It's a gentle way to nurture your body and mind, fostering a deeper connection.

Let's start with some basic mindful stretching exercises. One of my favorites is the gentle neck and shoulder stretch. Begin by sitting comfortably with your back straight. Slowly tilt your head to one side, bringing your ear towards your shoulder. Hold the stretch for a few breaths, feeling the gentle pull along the side of your neck. Repeat on the other side. Next, try the seated forward bend. Sit with your legs extended straight in front of you. Inhale deeply, then exhale as you gently reach for your toes, allowing your spine to lengthen. This stretch can help relieve lower back tension. Another simple yet effective stretch is the standing side stretch. Stand with your feet hip-width apart, raise your arms overhead, and clasp your hands together. Gently lean to one side, feeling the stretch along your side body. Hold for a few breaths, then switch sides.

Incorporating these stretches into your daily routine can make a significant difference in how you feel. Start your day with a morning stretching routine to awaken your body and mind. Spend a few minutes stretching as soon as you get out of bed, focusing on how each movement feels. Midday stretches can be a great way to relieve work-related tension. If you spend long hours at a desk, take short breaks to stretch your neck, shoulders, and back. These moments of mindfulness can refresh your mind and reduce stress. Consider a gentle stretching session in the evening to unwind and prepare for a restful sleep. Combining stretches with deep breathing can help you release the day's tension and promote relaxation.

Advanced mindful stretching exercises offer additional benefits for those looking to deepen their practice. Yoga-inspired stretches like the cat-cow or child's pose can provide deeper relaxation and flexibility. In the cat-cow pose, you move between arching and rounding your spine while synchronizing your breath with each movement. This dynamic stretch enhances spinal flexibility and promotes mindfulness through breath awareness. Dynamic stretching combined with mindful breathing can further enhance the mind-body connection. For example, flowing through gentle movements while focusing on your breath can create a meditative state, reducing stress and increasing mindfulness.

Partner stretching can also be a wonderful way to enhance connection and support. When you stretch with a partner, you rely on each other for balance and stability, fostering trust and communication. This practice can especially benefit couples or friends looking to deepen their bond through shared mindfulness. One simple partner stretch is the seated forward bend with a partner. Sit facing each other with your legs extended and feet touching. Hold each other's hands and take turns gently pulling each other forward into a stretch. Communication is key; ensure you're comfortable and supportive throughout the movement.

Mindful stretching is a versatile practice that can fit seamlessly into your daily life. Whether you're looking to relieve physical tension, reduce stress, or simply take a few moments for yourself, these exercises offer a holistic approach to well-being. By paying attention to your body and staying present in the moment, you can cultivate a sense of inner peace and connection that extends beyond the physical benefits of stretching. So, take a deep breath, stretch mindfully, and embrace this practice's calm and clarity.

Inclusivity in Mindfulness Practices

Inclusivity in mindfulness practices is about creating a space where everyone feels welcome, respected, and valued. It means acknowledging and honoring the diverse backgrounds, experiences, and perspectives that individuals bring to their mindfulness journey. By fostering an inclusive environment, we can enrich our mindfulness practice and build a supportive community that benefits everyone. Inclusivity allows us to learn from each other, share our unique insights, and grow together. It's about creating a space where everyone feels seen and heard, regardless of background or beliefs.

Diverse perspectives in mindfulness practice offer a wealth of benefits. We can draw on a broader range of wisdom and techniques when we include different spiritual and cultural traditions. This diversity can deepen our understanding and enhance our practice. For example, incorporating elements from Buddhist, Hindu, Christian, Indigenous, and other spiritual traditions can provide new insights and approaches to mindfulness. Using inclusive language in mindfulness instruction is also crucial. It ensures that everyone feels welcome and respected, regardless of their background. This might mean avoiding jargon or specific religious terminology and instead using language that is accessible and inviting to all.

Creating an inclusive mindfulness space involves thoughtful attention to the physical and emotional environment. Start by creating a space that reflects diverse cultural elements, such as artwork, symbols, or objects from different traditions. This can create a sense of belonging and respect for all participants. Ensuring accessibility for individuals with disabilities is also vital. This might include providing seating options, ensuring physical access, and offering materials in different formats, such as Braille or large print. Promoting belonging through mindful community activities can help everyone feel included. Organize events or practices that invite people to share their unique perspectives and experiences. This could be as simple as a sharing circle where everyone has the opportunity to speak or more structured activities like workshops or cultural celebrations.

Mindfulness can also be a powerful tool for promoting social justice and inclusivity. By practicing mindfulness in activism, we can approach social justice work with compassion, clarity, and resilience. Techniques such as mindful listening and holding space for others can foster empathy and understanding. Guided meditations focused on empathy and compassion can help us connect with others' experiences and motivations, deepening our commitment to social justice. Personal stories of using mindfulness for social change illustrate its potential. For example, one activist found that mindfulness helped her stay grounded and focused during protests, allowing her to respond to challenges calmly and clearly. Another used mindfulness to navigate difficult conversations about race and privilege, fostering deeper understanding and connection.

Ultimately, inclusivity in mindfulness practices creates a space where everyone can thrive. It's about embracing diversity, honoring different perspectives, and building a supportive, compassionate community. Whether practicing alone or with others, strive to create an inclusive environment that welcomes and respects everyone. This enriches your practice and builds a stronger, more connected community. By incorporating diverse perspectives, using inclusive language, creating accessible spaces, and promoting social justice, we can make mindfulness a truly inclusive practice. This approach benefits individuals and strengthens the community, fostering connections and promoting well-being for all.

Building a Supportive Community

The role of the community in maintaining holistic well-being cannot be overstated. Social support is a crucial factor in mental and physical health. Having a network of people who understand and support you can significantly reduce feelings of stress and loneliness. Studies have shown that strong social connections can improve immune function, lower rates of anxiety and depression, and even increase longevity. Mindfulness naturally fosters these connections by encouraging empathy and understanding. Mindfulness can strengthen bonds, enhance emotional resilience, and create a shared sense of purpose when practiced within a community.

Creating a mindful community starts with organizing groups and meetups where people can practice mindfulness. This could be as simple as a weekly meditation session at a local park or a more structured group that meets regularly to discuss mindfulness topics and share experiences. Facilitating mindful group activities is essential for nurturing these communities. Begin with a group check-in where everyone can share their current state of mind. Follow it with a guided meditation or a mindfulness exercise, such as mindful walking or eating. Ensure each session ends with a reflection period where participants can discuss their experiences and insights.

Settling guidelines for a supportive and inclusive community is crucial. Establish norms that promote respect, empathy, and non-judgment. Encourage open communication and create a safe space where everyone feels heard and valued. These guidelines help maintain a positive and nurturing environment, allowing the community to thrive. When everyone understands and respects the group's principles, it creates a foundation of trust and mutual support. This foundation is vital for the community's resilience, especially during challenging times.

Mindful communication within the community is another essential aspect. Practicing active listening in group settings can significantly strengthen connections. Encourage participants to listen fully without interrupting, reflecting on what they've heard to ensure understanding. This practice fosters deeper empathy and reduces misunderstandings. Techniques for expressing emotions mindfully can also enhance communication. Encourage members to use "I" statements to share their feelings and needs, which can help prevent conflicts and promote open dialogue. When conflicts arise, mindful dialogue can be an effective tool for resolution. This involves staying present, focusing on the issue at hand, and approaching the conversation with an open and non-judgmental mindset.

Sustaining community engagement over time requires regular check-ins and reflections. Schedule periodic reviews to assess the group's progress and address any challenges. These check-ins can help keep everyone aligned with the community's goals and ensure the group remains supportive and inclusive. Planning mindful events and retreats can also sustain engagement. Organize activities like weekend retreats, workshops, or mindfulness-themed social events to deepen connections and provide growth opportunities. These events can offer a break from daily routines and create memorable shared experiences that strengthen the community bond.

Another effective strategy is creating online platforms for ongoing support and connection. Use social media groups, forums, or messaging apps to maintain communication between meetups. These platforms can be spaces for sharing resources, offering support, and continuing discussions. They also allow members who cannot attend in-person meetings to stay connected. Regularly updating these platforms with new content and encouraging active participation can keep the community engaged and vibrant.

Building a supportive community through mindfulness practices enhances well-being on multiple levels. It fosters social connections, empathy, and resilience, providing a strong foundation for individual and collective growth. You can create a vibrant community that nurtures everyone involved by organizing mindful groups, facilitating activities, setting supportive guidelines, practicing mindful communication, and sustaining engagement. This holistic approach benefits each member and strengthens the community as a whole, promoting a sense of belonging and shared purpose.

Conclusion

As we end our journey together, I want to remind you of the vision that inspired this book: empowering you to cultivate emotional balance, inner calm, and self-acceptance through mindfulness. It's been a heartfelt mission to provide you with tools and techniques to help lighten the heavy loads of perfectionism, anxiety, and control. I hope that you feel more equipped to embrace peace in your daily life.

Throughout the chapters, we've explored various aspects of mindfulness and how it can transform your relationship with yourself and the world around you. We started with the power of self-compassion, learning how to treat ourselves with the same kindness we offer others. We delved into the basics of mindfulness, understanding its principles and the science behind it.

We discussed practical techniques like mindful breathing, body scan, and walking meditation, which are simple yet powerful practices that ground you in the present moment. We addressed specific challenges like managing anxiety, overcoming negative self-talk, and balancing multiple roles, each with tailored mindfulness exercises to make these tasks more manageable.

One of the key takeaways is that mindfulness is more than achieving perfection or always being calm. It's about being present and aware, accepting whatever arises with an open heart. It's about recognizing that it's okay to have flaws and that these imperfections make us human. It's about finding moments of peace amidst the chaos and learning to be gentle with ourselves in times of struggle.

Another important point is the interconnectedness of our mental, emotional, and physical well-being. Practicing mindfulness can strengthen this mind-body connection, leading to improved health and a deeper sense of fulfillment. Techniques like mindful stretching and body scan meditation can help you become more attuned to your body's signals, promoting overall wellness.

As you continue on this path, remember that mindfulness is a journey, not a destination. It's not about doing it perfectly but about showing up consistently. The practices and exercises we've covered are tools for your toolbox. Use them regularly, and they will become second nature. Integrate them into your daily routine through mindful mornings, mindful work breaks, or evening wind-downs.

I encourage you to take specific actions to maintain your mindfulness practice. Set aside a few minutes each day for meditation or mindful breathing. Create a dedicated space in your home to retreat for a moment of calm. Join a mindfulness group or community to share your experiences and gain support. Reflect on your progress through journaling and celebrate your small victories along the way.

I am deeply grateful to you for embarking on this journey with me and for allowing this book to be part of your path toward inner peace. Your willingness to explore these practices and make them a part of your life is truly inspiring.

Remember, you are not alone in this journey. We all face challenges and have moments of doubt and struggle. But we can find strength, resilience, and a sense of peace through mindfulness. Embrace your imperfections because they are what make you unique. Find joy in the present moment, even in the simplest of things. Continue cultivating emotional resilience and inner peace, knowing that every step you take is toward a more balanced and fulfilling life.

Keep going, keep practicing, and keep believing in yourself. You have everything you need within you to create a life of emotional balance and inner calm. And whenever you need a reminder or a bit of encouragement, this book will always be here for you.

With heartfelt gratitude and warmest wishes,

EveMeadows

References

- *Self-Compassion Research by Kristin Neff* https://self-compassion.org/the-research/
- *The Role of Self-Compassion in Development: A Healthier ...* https://www.ncbi.nlm.nih.gov/pmc/articles/PMC2790748/
- *The Five Myths of Self-Compassion* https://greatergood.berkeley.edu/article/item/the_five_myths_of_self_compassion
- *10 Ways to Overcome Perfectionism – Oregon Counseling* https://oregoncounseling.com/article/10-ways-to-overcome-perfectionism/
- *When science meets mindfulness - Harvard Gazette* https://news.harvard.edu/gazette/story/2018/04/harvard-researchers-study-how-mindfulness-may-change-the-brain-in-depressed-patients/
- *Neural mechanisms of mindfulness and meditation* https://www.ncbi.nlm.nih.gov/pmc/articles/PMC4109098/
- *Mindfulness and Emotion Regulation: Insights from ...* https://www.ncbi.nlm.nih.gov/pmc/articles/PMC5337506/
- *Communicating Mindfully in Relationships* https://www.psychologytoday.com/us/blog/conscious-communication/201709/communicating-mindfully-in-relationships
- *Mindful Breathing: Benefits, Types, and Scripts* https://psychcentral.com/health/mindful-breathing
- *Body Scan Meditation: Benefits and How to Do It* https://www.verywellmind.com/body-scan-meditation-why-and-how-3144782
- *Walking Meditation* https://www.headspace.com/meditation/walking-meditation
- *Mindful Eating: The Art of Presence While You Eat - PMC* https://www.ncbi.nlm.nih.gov/pmc/articles/PMC5556586/
- *How to Use Mindfulness Therapy for Anxiety: 15 Exercises* https://positivepsychology.com/mindfulness-for-anxiety/
- *8 Breathing Exercises for Anxiety You Can Try Right Now* https://www.healthline.com/health/breathing-exercises-for-anxiety
- *30 Grounding Techniques to Quiet Distressing Thoughts* https://www.healthline.com/health/grounding-techniques
- *From Chaos to Calm: How to Create a Zen Space at Home ...* https://marblewellness.com/post/from-chaos-to-calm-how-to-create-a-zen-space-at-home-for-anxiety-relief/

- *How to Identify and Manage Your Emotional Triggers* https://www.healthline.com/health/mental-health/emotional-triggers
- *Mindfulness and Emotion Regulation: Insights from …* https://www.ncbi.nlm.nih.gov/pmc/articles/PMC5337506/
- *Cognitive-Behavioral Treatments for Anxiety and Stress- …* https://www.ncbi.nlm.nih.gov/pmc/articles/PMC8475916/
- *The Relationship Between Mindfulness and Resilience* https://psychcentral.com/lib/mindfulness-the-art-of-cultivating-resilience
- *The Toxic Effects of Negative Self-Talk* https://www.verywellmind.com/negative-self-talk-and-how-it-affects-us-4161304
- *Cognitive Restructuring: Techniques and Examples* https://www.healthline.com/health/cognitive-restructuring
- *Exercise 2: Self-Compassion Break* https://self-compassion.org/exercises/exercise-2-self-compassion-break/
- *Mental Health Journaling: The Benefits of Writing for …* https://dayoneapp.com/blog/mental-health-journaling/
- *Toward a realistic approach to Mindfulness and Time …* https://connect.mayoclinic.org/blog/mindfulness-in-health/newsfeed-post/toward-a-realistic-approach-to-mindfulness-and-time-management/
- *Compassionate Boundaries: How to Say No with Heart* https://www.mindful.org/compassionate-boundaries-say-no-heart/
- *Parenting-focused mindfulness intervention reduces stress …* https://www.ncbi.nlm.nih.gov/pmc/articles/PMC7962755/
- *Relieve Stress with These 8 Tips for Creating a Mindful …* https://www.psychedconsult.com/relieve-stress-with-these-8-tips-for-creating-a-mindful-space-in-the-home/
- *Here and now: Discover the benefits of being present* https://www.betterup.com/blog/how-to-be-present
- *How to Use Mindfulness Therapy for Anxiety: 15 Exercises* https://positivepsychology.com/mindfulness-for-anxiety/
- *How to Forgive Yourself With Self-Compassion* https://www.psychologytoday.com/us/blog/striving-thriving/202207/how-forgive-yourself-self-compassion
- *Tips, Practices, and Activities for Mindful Communication* https://www.mindfulteachers.org/blog/mindful-communication
- *Meditation: A simple, fast way to reduce stress* https://www.mayoclinic.org/tests-procedures/meditation/in-depth/meditation/art-20045858
- *The Transformative Effects of Mindful Self-Compassion* https://www.mindful.org/the-transformative-effects-of-mindful-self-compassion/

- *Brief Mindfulness Meditation Improves Emotion Processing* https://www.ncbi.nlm.nih.gov/pmc/articles/PMC6795685/
- *How to Use Meditation for Better Sleep* https://www.healthline.com/health/meditation-for-sleep
- *Present Tense: 7 Mindfulness Strategies to Cope with Loss* https://www.healthline.com/health/mind-body/mindfulness-strategies-to-cope-with-loss
- *Communicating Mindfully in Relationships* https://www.psychologytoday.com/us/blog/conscious-communication/201709/communicating-mindfully-in-relationships
- *Use mindfulness to cope with chronic pain* https://www.mayoclinichealthsystem.org/hometown-health/speaking-of-health/use-mindfulness-to-cope-with-chronic-pain
- *30 Grounding Techniques to Quiet Distressing Thoughts* https://www.healthline.com/health/grounding-techniques
- *How To Create A Mindful Morning Routine* https://www.thegoodtrade.com/features/creating-a-mindful-morning-routine/
- *Transform Your Daily Commute (10 Mindful Techniques for a ...* https://moveinsync.medium.com/10-techniques-for-mindful-commuting-a5cb8aae0f36
- *How to Manage Stress with Mindfulness and Meditation* https://www.mindful.org/how-to-manage-stress-with-mindfulness-and-meditation/
- *Evening Meditation: Your Path to Stress-Free Nights* https://blog.mindvalley.com/evening-meditation/
- *Mind–body research moves towards the mainstream - NCBI* https://www.ncbi.nlm.nih.gov/pmc/articles/PMC1456909/
- *MINDFUL STRETCHINGGUIDE* https://uhs.berkeley.edu/sites/default/files/wellness-mindfulstretchingguide.pdf
- *3 Mindfulness Practices for Neurodiverse Meditators* https://www.mindful.org/3-mindfulness-practices-for-neurodiverse-meditators/
- *Section 8. Mindfulness and Community Building* https://ctb.ku.edu/en/table-of-contents/spirituality-and-community-building/mindfulness-community-building/main

Your Help Can Bring Peace to Someone's Life

"WHEN WE GIVE CHEERFULLY AND ACCEPT GRATEFULLY, EVERYONE IS BLESSED." - MAYA ANGELOU

Hey there!

If you've made it this far in *Women Embracing Peace*, I hope you've found the tools and stories within these pages as empowering and transformative as I intended. You and I have been on this journey together, finding ways to embrace mindfulness, inner calm, and self-compassion. Now, I need your help ensuring this book reaches the women who most need it.

I have a quick question for you: Would you help someone you've never met, even if you never received credit for it?

This person might be just like you were before you started this journey—overwhelmed, anxious, and searching for peace. She's juggling too much and feeling like she's falling short. She's looking for guidance but doesn't know where to start. Your experience could be the key to her breakthrough.

Most people judge a book by its cover... and its reviews. So here's my simple ask:

Please help women like her by leaving a review for *Women Embracing Peace*.

It won't cost a dime and will take less than 60 seconds, but it can impact another woman's life. Your review could help:

- One more woman break free from perfectionism.
- One more mother find balance in her hectic life.
- One more person discover the peace that mindfulness brings.
- One more reader regain hope and self-compassion.

To spread the calm, you only have to share your thoughts. It's quick, simple, and can help many others start their journey toward peace. Just click the link or scan the QR code below to leave your review.

If you love helping others (and I know you do!), you're exactly the person I want to connect with. Your review is the first step in helping more women join our community of peace-seekers, and together, we can spread the lessons of mindfulness, balance, and hope.

I'm so excited to keep walking this path with you and to hear how you've embraced peace through the practices in this book. Thank you from the bottom of my heart for being part of this journey.

Your biggest fan,

Eve Meadows

P.S. Sharing your review could be the difference between someone staying stuck in stress or finding the peace she's been searching for. If you think this book can help another woman, pass it along! You never know who might need it next.

www.ingramcontent.com/pod-product-compliance
Lightning Source LLC
Chambersburg PA
CBHW061302120726
48001CB00001B/439